What people are saying about …

She Smiles without Fear

"Do you sometimes feel that life's current circumstances, combined with the uncertainty of the future, can threaten to knock the joy right out of your heart and cause panic to saturate your soul? Katy McCown has unearthed the answer to this distressing condition and has crafted a practical resource to help us learn to settle our souls. *She Smiles without Fear* takes an in-depth dive into Scripture while also providing engaging anecdotes from her own journey with Jesus. This useful tool will not only empower you to smile confidently at the future, it will enable you to experience God's peace in the present."

Karen Ehman, *New York Times*–bestselling author, speaker with Proverbs 31 Ministries

"*She Smiles without Fear* invites women to rethink the stereotype of the Proverbs 31 woman being poised, planned, and perfect. Katy helped me learn through this study to exhale, shifting from "doing" to "being" with Jesus. I discovered that so much of my fear of the future is a *misplaced perspective of where I look for my future.* This book was my much-needed reset button that challenged me to refocus my gaze off my fears and onto the One who holds my future."

Lisa Allen, executive director of ministry & staff development at Proverbs 31 Ministries

"Having been through a painful divorce and facing a cavern of unknowns, I know all too well how fear of present circumstances and an uncertain future can grip our hearts so tightly it's hard to breath, much less trust God is in control. *She Smiles without Fear* gives a fresh, Scripture-based perspective on how, regardless of where our fears are rooted or what our circumstances are, getting our hearts right with God is the answer to reclaiming our peace and joy. Through Katy's inspirational stories, encouragement, tips, and action steps, every reader will feel lighter and happier once she completes the study."

Tracie Miles, author of *Living Unbroken* plus four bestselling
books, director of Compel Training at Proverbs 31 Ministries

"At Proverbs 31 Ministries, we've spent decades helping women see that the Proverbs 31 woman is not a standard of perfection or an object of comparison for us. It wasn't her activity that mattered the most—but rather her identity. A Proverbs 31 woman is, at her core, someone who seeks the Lord in everything she does and trusts Him wholeheartedly with her life. I love that Katy hones in on one key aspect of the Proverbs 31 woman that many women struggle with: fear of the future. With Katy's help, women will walk away from this five-week study hopeful and understanding that while we may feel afraid, we don't have to live in fear. I can't think of a better resource for right now!"

Lysa TerKeurst, #1 *New York Times*–bestselling
author, president of Proverbs 31 Ministries

"With what can seem like the weight of the world on our shoulders, we are all prone to letting 'overwhelm' creep in and snuff out the delight of life. *She Smiles without Fear* helps us understand what the word *joy* actually means and discover all God has for us when we really learn to look to Him. With highly practical steps, one of my very favorite writers, Katy McCown, invites us to journey alongside her to find the peace and joy we've always longed for, equipping us to finally face our future without fear!"

Ruth Schwenk, founder of TheBetterMom.com, cohost of *Rootlike
Faith* podcast, coauthor of *In a Boat in the Middle of a Lake*

"The Proverbs 31 woman is one of the most mysterious women in the Bible to us modern-day women. I love that Katy McCown is making her less mysterious through this fantastic Bible study. Katy is so wise and funny, and she helps women connect to the Word in a powerful way!"

Nicki Koziarz, bestselling author, speaker with Proverbs 31 Ministries

"Join Katy as she takes you on a journey to 'living sure' even when the future is not. Katy equips you with biblical wisdom and practical tools to turn your attention away from the what-ifs and worries of tomorrow so you can walk securely into your God-given assignments of today. You will walk away from this study with a strong, confident, purposeful, more intentional heart rooted in the deep and abiding love of Jesus."

Wendy Blight, author, biblical content specialist
for Proverbs 31 Online Bible Studies

"Katy McCown speaks to my heart every time I spend time with her. This book is no different. I was drawn in by the stories and given a secure footing to move forward by the truth she shares. If you struggle with fear and worry (don't we all?), you need the words on these pages."

Jill Savage, author of *Real Moms ... Real Jesus*
and *No More Perfect Marriages*

"When I first met Katy, we were both in the thick of newborns, young kids, and moving to a new city. Football brought us together, but our hearts keep our friendship alive. This study will truly encourage you to uncover what is holding you back from becoming the woman God longs for you to be. Throughout this book you will think, pray, learn, and definitely laugh. Thank you, Katy, for taking the time to help all of us laugh."

Kirsten Watson, disciple, wife of NFL athlete/
author Benjamin Watson, mother of seven

"Katy McCown is uniquely gifted with a passionate voice that inspires you to know God more. I've had the privilege of sitting around the table as she teaches about becoming more like Jesus. In *She Smiles without Fear*, you'll feel like Katy is sitting around the table with you, too, as she shares stories from her family and faith. This study will equip you to find freedom from your fear of the future and a fresh infusion of joy-filled faith."

Barb Roose, speaker, author of *Surrendered, Joshua,* and *I'm Waiting, God*

She
Smiles
Without
Fear

KATY MCCOWN

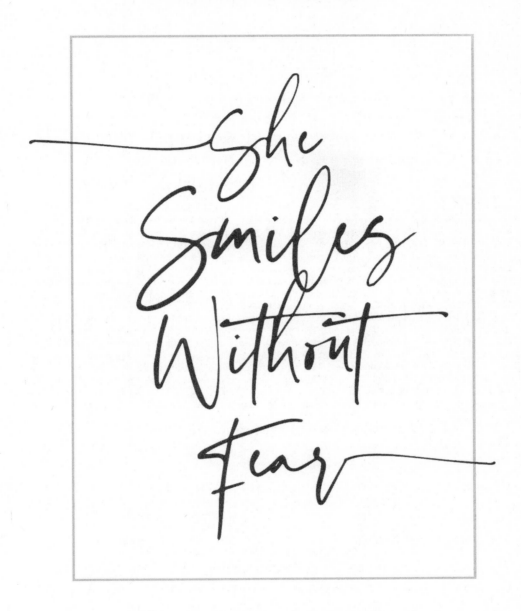

She Smiles Without Fear

Proverbs 31 for Every Woman

DAVID C COOK

transforming lives together

SHE SMILES WITHOUT FEAR
Published by David C Cook
4050 Lee Vance Drive
Colorado Springs, CO 80918 U.S.A.

Integrity Music Limited, a division of David C Cook
Brighton, East Sussex BN1 2RE, England

The graphic circle C logo is a registered trademark of David C Cook.

ISBN 978-0-8307-8137-9
eISBN 978-0-8307-8138-6

The Team: Susan McPherson, Jeff Gerke, Judy Gillispie, Jon Middel,
Kayla Fenstermaker, Susan Murdock
Cover Design: John Spriggs

Printed in the United States of America
First Edition 2021

1 2 3 4 5 6 7 8 9 10

102020

To Mom,
for leading me to Jesus
and showing me what it looks like
to live every day clothed in
His strength and dignity.

Meet the Author

Katy McCown is president of She Laughs Ministries, a writer for Proverbs 31 Ministries, and a national speaker. Katy's Bible teaching days began in her home as a young adult. From the floor of her children's bedroom to the living room where she gathered with other women, Katy has spent more than a decade opening God's Word and teaching it to others. In 2017, Katy joined the First 5 team at Proverbs 31 Ministries, where she continues to study, train, and teach the Bible.

Katy is married to former NFL quarterback Luke McCown. She left her job as a television news reporter to join him on his adventure in the National Football League. During his thirteen years in the NFL, they moved more than a dozen times as Luke played on six teams, primarily as a backup quarterback. Through all the uncertainties and surprises, Katy has learned some things about "living sure" even when the future is not, because even when God's path seemed to sideline her plans, it never sidelined her purpose..

Luke and Katy have six children, plus two puppies and a cat (who they are pretty sure thinks he's a dog). Katy loves a cup of strong coffee—or two—and her van is never clean. Never ever.

Connect with Katy at www.katymccown.com.

*Strength and dignity
are her clothing,
and she smiles
at the future.*

Proverbs 31:25 NASB

Contents

Week 4: Her Heart's Pursuit: Living Directed

Week 5: My Heart's Perspective: Living Intentional

Introduction

I Didn't See That Coming

I knew I needed help.

I needed to stop, but nothing in my mind seemed to be communicating with my body. My mouth wouldn't open. My voice wouldn't scream. My arms wouldn't straighten out to catch my quickly falling self. Any minute now, my face would become closely acquainted with the concrete below. This was happening.

But let me back up a little.

Just a few hours earlier, Luke and I had shuffled to the car for what had the makings of a perfect night. With six little ones, we didn't get out much, and when we did, it was usually just to go down the road to a local restaurant and try to stay out long enough for the sitter to get the kids in bed.

But not tonight. For weeks we'd planned a bit of a road trip to have dinner with friends and catch a college basketball game. Not that I'm much of a college basketball fan, but when I married a football player, I figured sports would somehow work their way into many a date night. And just as I expected, they did.

We ate a good dinner, then drove to the stadium, where I stepped out of the car onto the rocky parking area. Immediately I realized I'd worn the wrong shoes. For starters, I couldn't even see the large building at which the aforementioned basketball game was being played. There was sure to be a hike to the door, and I had on heels. High heels.

In my defense, I have a mental situation in which I stand about five inches taller in my head than I do in real life. I didn't realize I was "divinely created to be on the front row of pictures," as my friend Amanda says, until I married a man well over six feet tall. So, in order to get my real-life height to match the height in my head, I wear heels just about everywhere I go.

I recently switched to wedges for the sake of my ankles and, well, to save myself from falling. But on this night I'd worn stilettos. Stilettos to walk a mile to a basketball game.

So here we go.

It was a nice night, which meant that, no matter how inconvenient my shoe choice was, we could take our time. I looped my arm around Luke's, and off we went on our spring-evening stroll.

That lasted seven steps.

It was at this point that the sky lit up in front of us. It wasn't supposed to do that. It was full-on nighttime. The sky was supposed to be black, but instead, it turned white. Lightning flashed to alert us of a coming storm.

And that was a real problem because my shirt could not get wet. It was the kind of material that, if it got wet, would never dry. I'd spend the rest of the night soaked, cold, and miserable while everyone else enjoyed a basketball game. Nope. My shirt could not get wet. So much for the stroll—we needed to get moving.

"Whoa," I said to Luke as all this flooded my thoughts, "we should walk faster." You can imagine my surprise when he all but brushed off my concern. He replied something to the effect of "We're fine" and continued at his casual pace.

Excuse me? We're fine? Every few minutes the lightning flashed again to prove the storm was inching closer and closer and closer. With no time to talk, I devised a genius plan.

I once heard that when you train a dog to walk on a leash, the goal is to get it to walk just about a half step behind you. (Stay with me here.) You set the pace, and the dog adjusts its speed to keep in step with you. I decided I would try to apply this same principle to Luke. I gradually increased my speed, hoping that my arm looped through his would keep him in step with me and he wouldn't even notice. And it worked!

The pace of my heart far outraced the pace of my feet, but nevertheless we had almost made it to the entrance of the stadium. By this time I had drawn some conclusions about the looming storm. One, it was moving toward us even faster than I'd thought. And two, this storm would afford us no warning drizzle. It was clear this was a soaker storm. There would be no period of scattered raindrops before the bottom fell out of the clouds, so a person wishing not to get wet had better be inside before the first drop fell.

And then it happened.

I felt the first drop.

Now, remember that whole thing about no warning raindrops and how my shirt could not get wet. There was really only one option left. I turned to the rest of the group and announced what I knew every one of them must be thinking: "Let's run!"

I didn't wait for an answer. I pivoted on the toes of the heels that made me tall in the shirt that couldn't get wet, and I darted toward the door in a sprint that must have rivaled that of an Olympian.

Two or three strides into my sprint, just as I approached full speed, I collided with a cement post.

Clearly I hadn't seen the post. It was about hip high, and my eyes had been fixed on the door that led to the dry arena. Unfortunately the post didn't completely stop me. It more or less redirected me straight toward the ground.

Which brings us to the part where I couldn't make my body do what I knew it should do.

About the time I'd reconciled myself to the fact that a meeting between me and the ground was a sure thing, I felt a strong, solid arm wrap around my waist.

The hand gripped me and lifted me, reversing the effects of my fall. Cradled in the strength of this arm, I found myself standing upright and unharmed. My husband had rescued me.

Now before you go getting all emotional about Luke's chivalrous act, I should tell you that I don't think his motivation was to save me so much as to stop the madness that was happening around his wife.

One piece of advice before we move on from this moment. If you ever find yourself in a similar situation, I have four words for you: Don't. Make. Eye. Contact.

So there I was, safely back on my feet, not making eye contact, and so far still dry. I adjusted my sprint to be more of a speed walk to the door. Once inside, I took a slight detour to the bathroom to make sure I wasn't bleeding. I wasn't. Then I rejoined the group at our seats in the arena.

By this time the story had passed all the way down the row. One by one, friends and family asked, "Are you okay?" I snapped back that I was fine, then melted into my seat next to Luke. He put his arm around my shoulders and pulled me close to whisper, "I told you it wasn't raining."

Thanks, babe.

As I recall that dreadful yet hysterical night, I'm challenged to take a good look at how I handle my fear of the future. That night, I was afraid of a literal thunderstorm that threatened to create physical discomfort and ruin my plans. But in my day-to-day life, fear can go a lot deeper than that.

With my thoughts fixed on fears of the future, sickness infects my hopes for loved ones. Failure invades the landscape of my dreams and goals. Moral decay lays a land mine for the hearts of my children. Natural disasters make me wonder if there's even a future to consider. I'm inclined to park my heart on one or all of these things.

I worry about not being prepared. I struggle to find the balance between reasonable responsibility and trusting God's provision. I don't want to be caught off guard by something awful. I'd rather try to orchestrate the events of my life so that my future plays a beautiful melody, free of disaster and despair.

What's so bad about that, anyway? Is it so terrible to want to avoid hardship if you can? I feel like, if I fix my eyes on the storm, I can handle it and maybe even avoid the downpour altogether.

But there's a problem with this approach, because when we fix our eyes on the future, it alters our actions in the present. We run into obstacles (sometimes in the form of cement posts) that could have easily been avoided. Worse, we miss out on the blessings happening right in front of us.

It takes work to stay one step ahead of the future. It demands our full attention. Meanwhile, in the present, we live paralyzed by fear, unable to enjoy the blessings right before us—much less engage in God's prearranged purposes for our lives. We're desperate to arrange the details of tomorrow yet hopeless because we sense we're losing today.

That's where I found myself one sunny afternoon. As the kids giggled down a waterslide and the wind rustled through the leaves, I choked back tears. Amid the beauty of everyday life, I couldn't wipe fear from my mind.

I needed an answer for my fears. I needed someone to tell me it was all going to be okay, no matter what. I needed somebody to tell me the future wouldn't be filled with my worst-case scenarios. But no one could.

Around that time I recorded this prayer in my journal:

> Jesus, I have these fears. Fears of the future. I'm scared. I know Your ways are
> not mine. I know they are good and far greater than anything I could fathom.
> I don't want to walk around shaky, anxious, fearful and distracted. Teach me
> how to live today.

Maybe you know what I'm talking about. It seems many of us are looking for an answer for our fears these days.

For decades fear has had a major impact on our world and how we live in it. More than twenty years ago, sociologists even gave the culture's condition a name. *Risk society* describes any culture "increasingly preoccupied with threats to safety, both real and perceived."[1] Fear has caused the decline of both mental and physical health. Depression, fatigue, heart problems, and intestinal issues can all be consequences of fear. Fear has also been linked to economic decline.[2]

And the church is not free from the effects of fear. At the time of this study's publication, the most popular verse on a well-known worldwide Bible app had something to do with fear or worry—for three years in a row.[3]

As women, we fear health problems and sudden disaster. We worry about the future and what it might hold for the people we love. We want to feel secure and confident, but we live paralyzed by the uncertainties of tomorrow.

The truth is that there is plenty to fear and it's not going anywhere. If anything, our reasons to fear seem to be growing larger and more threatening by the minute. That's why we're journeying through this Bible study together. We need an answer for our fear.

I can't change the future, but fear of the future can change me.

The only place I've found an answer for my fear is in God's Word. I want to share with you how the Bible can answer your fear too. In the weeks ahead, we will use the Proverbs 31 woman as a guide. The Bible describes her as a woman who "smiles at the future" without fear (v. 25 NASB). As we examine the Scriptures about her, you will learn five principles to apply to your own life to help you smile without fear of the future.

To smile without fear of the future, you need to:

1. Spend less time *doing* and more time *being* with Jesus.
2. Exchange the *fear of the future* for the *fear of the LORD*.
3. Rely on your Savior instead of yourself.
4. Pursue love.
5. Live faithful today.

As you learn to apply these steps to your life, I pray that you will be able to turn your attention from the what-ifs of tomorrow to invest in the God-given assignments of today and that you will build a future of confidence, security, and purpose. Here are a few things to help you as you work through this Bible study book:

- The first video session is an introductory session. After watching it, you'll begin your first week of personal study. To view the videos, just go to https://lesson-dl.com/ and use access code 1504639.
- Each week is divided into five days of personal study. Days 1–4 include a "Digging In" section designed to take you deeper into the subject we're discussing that day, and each day includes a "Work It Out" section to help you apply what you're learning.
- Day 5 is different from the other days. It introduces you to a biblical person or group who demonstrated the principle you studied that week. Day 5 is a little shorter, and you will be prompted to spend time journaling.
- Each week concludes with a video session. You can watch these sessions individually or in a group.
- Scripture quotations and fill-in-the-blanks come from the ESV translation of the Bible, unless otherwise noted.

Remember my irrational sprint-turned-flop at the basketball game? Well, guess what—it turns out it *did* rain that night. I'd like to take this moment to acknowledge that I was, in fact, right all along. The storm I feared did exactly what I thought it would do—it soaked the stadium.

But I didn't even know it.

It wasn't until the game ended and we stepped out onto wet ground that we realized it had rained. Everything I had feared had indeed come to pass—but when it did, I was sheltered securely under the stadium roof.

I can't change the future, but fear of the future can change me. It can twist me into something completely different from what God designed me to be and render me unavailable to invest in the moments happening right now.

I've decided I'm not okay with that.

What about you? Are you ready to step under God's shelter and start smiling without fear of the future? Me too. Just let me find some different shoes first.

Video Session 1:
Introduction

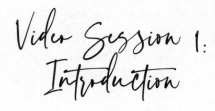

Watch video session 1, and use this space to write notes or record insights.

Week 1

There's a Heart behind This

Memory Verse

*Keep your heart with all vigilance, for
from it flow the springs of life.*

Proverbs 4:23

Introduction

They started small. So small, in fact, that we didn't really notice them. They blended into the walls.

We had lived in our home for several years when we began to notice cracks in the walls. A little wrinkle here, a small chip there—but barely visible and certainly nothing to be concerned about.

After a while, though, the cracks expanded, and we finally decided to do something about them. With a bit of plaster and paint, we patched them and went on with the business of daily life.

But the cracks soon returned. And they didn't just return—they kept growing. One crack turned into two, and two turned into ten. Pretty soon, everywhere we looked, we saw a crack. They showed up in more than one room. We found them in the kitchen and in bedrooms. They sliced through the frame above doors and even stretched to the ceiling. This project had become more than just a paint job.

It turned out that our attention had been on the wrong thing. We'd been thinking about what we saw happening on the surface of our home, when in reality something in the foundation was weak and needed to be fixed. The cracks weren't the problem—they were only a result of the problem.

After years of bearing the weight of our house, the beams holding it in place began to shift. That shifting caused everything to droop. As the foundation drooped, the walls and ceilings cracked.

We hired a crew of experts to come help us. They brought equipment and concrete blocks and disappeared underneath the house. It was tedious, loud, and grueling work. For hours the team manipulated materials to push back into place what years of settling had caused to sag. One block at a time, they lifted the floor back into a stable position.

It was only once the foundation was stabilized that we could successfully repair the cracks.

Day 1

Where Is This Coming From?

Memory Verse

Keep your heart with all vigilance, for from it flow the springs of life.
Proverbs 4:23

Since you're joining me for a study titled *She Smiles without Fear*, I'm going to assume you're either currently facing an uncertain future or you think you might be one day soon.

So before we go any further, let's talk about it. What are some things about your future that make you anxious? Use the space below to jot them down.

Several years ago, I posted a Bible verse to social media, and I was struck by the response. Women from different states, life stages, and cultures all agreed on one thing: they wanted the life this verse describes, but they weren't really sure it was possible.

This is the verse I posted:

Strength and dignity are her clothing,
and she smiles at the future. (Prov. 31:25 NASB)

Can I tell you my goal for this study? It might sound crazy to you, but I want you to hear it. By the end of these five weeks, I want you to be able to come back to this page and fill in the following blanks with your name:

Strength and dignity are _____ clothing, and
_____ smiles at the future.

I hope that excites you as much as it excites me!

I also know that being able to fill in these blanks may seem unlikely, if not impossible, to you. Believe me—I read the same news articles you read. I hear the same predictions and absorb the same devastating reports. I understand that it sounds unbelievable that you could look at the landscape of the world we occupy yet smile without fear of the future.

But I also know something else—God's Word is timeless. Its truth isn't only for a season or a specific time in history. It is still living and active and useful today (see Heb. 4:12).

With that in mind, let's get started.

This verse in Proverbs 31 is a part of a group of verses about an unnamed woman who has become known as the Proverbs 31 woman. As we begin this study, let's get a little better acquainted with her. Open your Bible or Bible app, and read Proverbs 31:10–31.

Write down some things you notice about this woman.

Using the following word bank, circle some of the ways your list makes you feel, or use the empty boxes to write some words of your own.

tired	inadequate	anxious
intrigued	defeated	hopeful
hesitant	expectant	optimistic

I'm guessing you compiled a pretty impressive list of phrases about the woman in Proverbs 31. Things like *she seeks, she rises, she considers,* and *she perceives.* If your hand wasn't tired from all that writing, you may have gone even further and recorded ideas like *she opens* and *she makes* and *she makes some more* and *she opens again.*

At first glance, the road to smiling without fear of the future might seem daunting. What are a spindle and distaff, anyway? But before you go searching the internet, let's look at these verses through a different lens.

DIGGING IN

The book of Proverbs focuses on the practical part of living out God's Word. It's a book about *how. How* do I obey God and follow Him in the ebb and flow of everyday life?

Read the following verse from 1 Samuel. Watch for what two things God told Samuel *not* to look at. What did God say He sees?

> The LORD said to Samuel, "Do not look on his appearance or on the height of
> his stature, because I have rejected him. For the LORD sees not as man sees: man
> looks on the outward appearance, but the LORD looks on the heart." (16:7)

In this chapter God had led the prophet Samuel to Bethlehem to anoint His chosen king for Israel, David. As Samuel surveyed the sons of Jesse, God instructed him about what would qualify the chosen one—his heart.

Throughout Scripture, the heart refers to the seat of our thoughts, emotions, and desires. It's the place where our intentions are formed, and as we just read, our hearts are what God sees when He looks at us.

Look up the verses below, and draw a line to match each with what it reveals about our hearts.

Jeremiah 17:9	Our hearts are deceitful.
Matthew 12:34	Springs of life flow from our hearts.
Luke 10:27	We can love God with our whole hearts.
Proverbs 4:23	With our hearts we believe in God.
Psalm 44:21	Our mouths speak the overflow of our hearts.
Romans 10:10	God knows the secrets of our hearts.

Physically, the heart is a vital organ. Without it, we would instantly die. There's absolutely no way to live without a beating heart. But the heart is vital not only to our physical lives but also to our spiritual lives. To live spiritually, we need more than just a beating heart—we need a holy heart. With our hearts we believe in God and love Him. Our hearts pour out truth or they seep lies. And from our hearts bubble springs of life.

How would your life be different if your heart produced springs of life?

God is far more interested in our motives than He is in our motions.

We could spend the next five weeks working hard to permeate our daily lives with all the activity we read about in Proverbs 31. But those motions will never lead our hearts to smile without fear of the future. Because, like with my house, what we see on the surface is often an indication of what's happening underneath. Sure, we can coat our lives with the plaster and paint of our to-do lists, but eventually we will have to deal with the failing foundation beneath our actions.

There's a heart behind this. For the woman in Proverbs 31 and for us. The smile we are here to find is not something we work our way into. It's something we receive as we respond to God.

> All a person's ways seem pure to them,
>   but motives are weighed by the LORD. (Prov. 16:2 NIV)

What does this verse say a person evaluates?

What does it say God evaluates?

God is far more interested in our motives than He is in our motions. Yes, our actions are important, and we will talk about the actions of the Proverbs 31 woman during our time together. But before we can produce actions that glorify God, we must have hearts positioned and conditioned to respond to Him.

Maybe your heart has spent years settling beneath the weight of sin or fear or the cares of this life. Maybe you've been exhausting yourself with daily plaster and paint, and you don't know whether you have any energy left to consider your heart. I won't lie to you—heart work is hard work. But that's why we're here. We can do this together.

Our faith hangs not on the future but on the One who holds the future.

God's Word will lift our hearts into a stable place and make us capable of standing in uncertain times. This heart work will be the foundation on which we build a future of security, confidence, and purpose.

As we close today, go back to Proverbs 31:10–31 and read it one more time. This time, look for the heart behind her actions. You can use the space below to jot down some ways this passage helps you see things differently or to record what you notice about her heart.

WORK IT OUT

At the end of each day, you'll find a section called "Work It Out." This will be a place for you to practically apply the things we're talking about.

As we start our first week together, I want you to ask God to reveal the condition of your heart. Think about how you might fill in the following blank:

She _____.

To help you know what word or words to use, consider how you might respond in this moment: You're expecting your husband (or friend, sister, mom, etc.) to meet you for dinner. You wait thirty minutes after the agreed-upon time, and he's still a no-show. What thoughts race through your head while you wait?

> **He's hurt.** *What route did he take to get here?* You check your phone for a missed call from a number you don't know and consider bolting for the car to retrace the path he would have driven to the restaurant. If this is where your mind goes, you might fill in the blank above so it reads something like "She worries," "She fears," or "She panics."

> **He doesn't care.** Your head drops, and a tear may even cloud your eye as you pick yourself apart and tear yourself to shreds. As you catalog all that you believe is wrong with you, you decide it's no wonder he's not here. If this is the conclusion you find yourself rushing to, you might fill in the blank so it reads "She compares" or "She doubts."

> **He's not worth it.** Your fingers drum the table as you run through the long list of demands still on your plate. *How dare he waste my time!* If this is how your thinking goes, you might fill in the blank so it reads "She erupts," "She controls," or "She guards."

Maybe you're like me, and at one time or another, you've responded all three ways. But there is good news!

In her book *Living So That*, Wendy Blight wrote, "Emotionally, our faith is often muddled by fear, hesitancy, and doubt. But our feelings become irrelevant when Jesus is the object of our faith—when He alone is the One in whom we trust."[1]

Our faith hangs not on the future but on the One who holds the future. What we do this week will solidify your faith and lay a firm foundation on which you can stand in uncertain times. I'm on the edge of my seat, and I hope you are too!

The First Step to Smiling without Fear

Memory Verse

Keep your _Heart_ with all vigilance, for from it flow the springs of life.
Proverbs 4:23

It's as though the worn-out piece of wood can tell the future.

Years of use have literally left their mark on the old stick, and each time it appears, anticipation swirls in the hearts of my little people.

During the days of my husband's youth, as he and his siblings grew in age and size, Luke's mom took a wooden board and made it a measuring stick. Year after year, Luke and his brothers and sister would scoot their heels all the way to the wall, stretch their necks as long as they could make them, and wait anxiously to see the new line that marked how much they had grown.

Now, decades later, my children like to measure themselves on this same old piece of wood. Mostly because my husband and his brothers now stand over six feet tall ... and possibly because two of them played more than ten years of professional football.

So when my boys scoot their heels all the way to the wall and stretch their necks as long as they can make them, they wait anxiously to find out if their line today matches the line of their daddy or uncles all those years ago. Because if it does, then their dreams of being tall or perhaps even of being a professional athlete seem more likely to come true.

We all have a tool by which we measure ourselves. That one person or thing that makes us believe what we've done, how we look, or how we live is a success or a failure.

Maybe it's the woman at church who somehow shows up on time every single Sunday. Her makeup is on, her hair is combed (or even curled), every one of her children have on shoes, and nothing falls out of her car when she opens the door.

Or maybe it's the woman at the gym who sits on the Spin bike next to you every Tuesday and Thursday. She doesn't sweat … she glistens. Nothing jiggles, and she always has a brand-new, made-from-scratch, straight-from-the-farm recipe to share.

Maybe it's the girl at work whose talent always seems to get noticed. Opportunities seem to fall in her lap, and doors fly open in front of her.

Maybe it's even this woman, the woman in Proverbs 31, whom you have set up as a measuring stick in your life. A standard that, deep down, you feel like you'll never come close to meeting.

Just between you and God, spend a few minutes considering the measuring sticks you've set up in your life. In the space below, write down some of the ways you compare yourself with others.

Read Proverbs 31:10: "An excellent wife who can find? She is far more precious than jewels."

I don't want you to get hung up on the word *wife* in this verse. Wherever you are—whether you're single and not even thinking about marriage, a widow learning how to be single for the second time, a woman happily married for decades, or a woman whose marriage has fallen apart before her eyes—this study and these Scriptures are for you.[1] As we go through each week together, you'll learn why, but for now, just trust me on this.

The twenty-two verses about the Proverbs 31 woman begin with *value*.

I don't willingly bring up grade school math class. I think that's something most of us would like to forget. But for just a minute, let's go back there. Do you remember the > and < signs? They are used for comparing numbers and expressions. They show when something is more than or less than something else. For example, 10 is more than 2, so we write $10 > 2$. Or to show that 5 is less than 10, we'd write $5 < 10$. *Whew!* Glad that's over.

Proverbs 31:10 also makes a comparison. Let's reread it, this time from a different translation: "A wife of noble character who can find? She is worth far more than rubies" (NIV). Did you catch the comparison? Based on our math lesson, it's saying, *her worth > rubies.*

The woman who smiles without fear is valued as being worth more than rubies. It actually says her worth is *far* more than rubies, but I don't think we have a sign for that.

Today rubies are fairly common, so to truly understand this comparison, we need to know a little more about rubies in Old Testament times.

Israel, where the author of Proverbs 31 lived, was not a land rich in precious stones. Consequently, stones were prized for their "qualities of rarity, beauty, hardness, color, brilliance, and durability."[2] In Scripture, the particular precious stone translated "rubies" in Proverbs 31:10 is compared with wisdom (see Job 28:18; Prov. 3:15; 8:11), and it was "possibly one of the precious stones in the high priest's breastplate" (see Ex. 28:17).[3]

Some scholars believe the verses about the Proverbs 31 woman were passed down from a mother to a son as she desired to weave into the fabric of her son's understanding what was good for him.[4]

While this comparison may have been shaped by a mother seeking to guide her son, God Himself has defined your value. Jesus even talked about the connection between value and security.

DIGGING IN

Look up and read Matthew 6:25–34.

Jesus opened these verses with an instruction. What is it? (v. 25) Do not worry

What two things did Jesus tell His listeners to look at? (v. 26, 28) *birds, flowers*

After Jesus told His audience to look at the birds, what question did He ask them? (v. 26)

Are you not more valuable than they

Read through these verses one more time, and count how many times Jesus said, "Do not be anxious." What did Jesus say to do instead of being anxious? (v. 33)

Seek first His kingdom

Your value is not based on ever-changing earthly measurements and comparisons. It's not defined by your place on the corporate ladder, the number of likes on your social media posts, or the cleanliness of your kitchen counter. Instead, your value is rooted in the unshakable, unchanging name of God. And as Jesus pointed out to His followers, your value to God is the catalyst to stop worrying and start seeking Him.

Read Ephesians 2:8–10.

By grace you have been saved through faith. And this is not your own doing; it is the gift of God, not a result of works, so that no one may boast. For we are his workmanship, created in Christ Jesus for good works, which God prepared beforehand, that we should walk in them.

How do you define *grace*?

If you've lived in Christian circles for very long, you've likely heard the word *grace*. If you haven't grown up in church, you may have heard this word too. In either case, you may have no idea what it really means.

Our culture's definition of *grace* is something like "elegance" or "poise." It refers to appearance or action. You might describe someone as acting gracious or looking graceful. It may also be synonymous with *kind*, *polite*, or *courteous*.

Christians define *grace* as the undeserved gift God gave us through Jesus. But the end goal of understanding grace is not the ability to recite its definition on demand. God's grace is something that should make every day of our lives different.

Look up the following verses, and fill in the blanks with what you learn about God's grace:

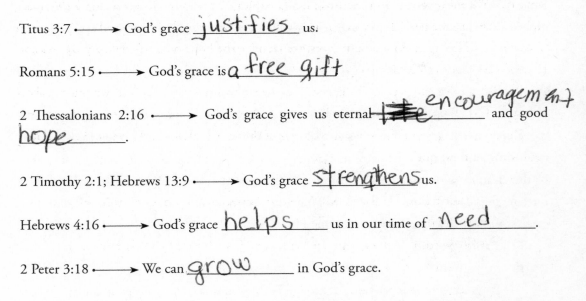

Titus 3:7 ———→ God's grace _justifies_ us.

Romans 5:15 ———→ God's grace is _a free gift_

2 Thessalonians 2:16 ———→ God's grace gives us eternal ~~life~~ _encouragement_ and good _hope_.

2 Timothy 2:1; Hebrews 13:9 ———→ God's grace _strengthens_ us.

Hebrews 4:16 ———→ God's grace _helps_ us in our time of _need_.

2 Peter 3:18 ———→ We can _grow_ in God's grace.

Does one of these verses stand out to you more than the others? If so, use the space below to write out the entire verse with its reference.

Hopefully, after reading through these verses, you have a better understanding of the riches of God's grace. But you may still be wondering what that has to do with value and how grace can enable you to smile without fear in the face of uncertainty.

Let's look at two pivotal shifts that occur when we receive God's grace and allow it to impact our daily lives.

First, God's grace defines us. The Greek word translated "workmanship" in Ephesians 2:10 is *poiēma*, and it describes us as the product of God's hand. The Amplified Bible says we are "His own master work, a work of art" (AMP).

In their daily devotional about the book of Proverbs, Timothy and Kathy Keller said this: "If we look to human beings more than to God for our worth and value, we will be trapped by anxiety."[5] When we look around at anyone or anything else to determine whether we measure up, we exchange the free gift of God's grace for the chains of performance-based acceptance. In the process of trying to do it all ourselves, we sacrifice the hope of God's divine purposes and plans for the traps of fear and failure.

Second, God's grace frees us. To become women who smile without fear, we must make a decision: Is it all up to God, or is it all up to me? And by *it*, I mean all of it—my future, my people, my plans, my pressures, my fears. Look at the list you made at the beginning of day 1, and consider these questions:

- If I can't trust God with what is most important to me, can I trust Him with anything?
- If I *can* trust God with my eternity, shouldn't I be able to trust Him with my future?

If it's all up to us, we will find no confidence in God's ability or willingness to guide and protect us. We'll live exhausted, confused, and afraid—constantly adjusting our efforts to match what we see around us and hoping we don't take a wrong turn that proves disastrous.

But if it is all up to God and His grace, if we truly believe that Jesus has defeated death and sin once and for all and that, by faith in Jesus, God extends to us the right to freely receive His grace and become coheirs to His kingdom, we'll stop trying so hard to impress God and will simply be impressed by Him.

This leads us to the very first step to becoming a woman who smiles without fear:

> ✤ **To smile without fear of the future, I need to spend less time *doing* and more time *being* with Jesus.** ✤

Maybe for you this feels like a relief. The idea that we could begin to become women who smile without fear simply by sitting with Jesus may bring a freedom you never thought could be so easily found. And, sister, I'm rejoicing with you today!

But for some, this step feels futile. You may be feeling a little edgy right now because this step doesn't seem like a step at all. You may think it could not possibly be enough to handle the fears you're facing today.

If that's you, sister, I want to tell you I understand. When it feels like there is so much to arrange, I'm the first in line to get it done. Activity soothes my anxieties because I feel like I'm moving toward a solution. So when I recommend sitting, although so much remains unresolved, I know it may feel unproductive, if not completely irresponsible. To you, sister, I want to say, please don't skip this step. There is activity to come, but before our activity can truly soothe our anxiety, we must first be deeply connected to Jesus.

Think of it this way—as long as you're sitting, you can't collide with a cement post. (Refer back to "I Didn't See That Coming" if you have no idea what I'm talking about.) Often the demands and expectations we place on ourselves flow from a desire to do all and be all for the people we love. We exhaust ourselves trying to give them the best and protect them from the worst, all the while worrying that we can't be all we should be for them.

The truth is, you're right. You can't be everything for your loved ones. But you were never supposed to be. If God's grace is sufficient for us, we can trust that it will also be sufficient for the people we love (see 2 Cor. 12:9).

If God's grace is sufficient for us, we can trust that it will also be sufficient for the people we love..

WORK IT OUT

> ✎ To smile without fear of the future, I need to spend less time *doing* and more time *being* with Jesus. ✎

Several years ago, a friend introduced me to a simple but powerful way to spend time with Jesus. It involved quieting myself and being still. I very much disliked her idea because, as I mentioned before, it felt futile and unproductive. But as she kept prompting me to do it—and I kept reluctantly obliging—I began to understand why she wanted me to do this. Because when I sat still, God met me in my quiet times with Him.

I want to encourage you to try something. At the end of each day this week, be still. Take two or three minutes and quiet your thoughts, your body, your phone, your television, and anything else that makes noise. Then sit with your heart fixed on Jesus. It's okay to set a timer on your phone.

It sounds easy enough, but you may find it difficult, especially in these first few days. After a matter of seconds, you may find yourself making a grocery list or scrolling through what you have to do when this time is over. You may start to fall asleep or hum a song you heard on the radio earlier in the day. And that's okay. Shake it off and refocus. A part of being still is practicing.

Remember, we're not even bringing our requests to God during this time. As you do this each day, you may end up setting that timer for longer and longer amounts of time with Jesus.

So let's put our first step into action. For the next few minutes, simply sit with Jesus. Use the space below to record any takeaways you have from this time.

_____

_____

_____

_____

Her worth > rubies.

Day 3

A Place Where You Can Be Safe

Memory Verse

Guard your *heart* with all

vigilance, for from it flow the springs of life.

Proverbs 4:23

I brushed my teeth but tried not to move. If I did, I might interrupt her.

I'd grown so fond of these moments. My baby girl, quickly gaining her independence, had made a habit of sitting on my feet. It might be while I cooked dinner or when I stood over the counter to consult my day planner or even sometimes while I brushed my teeth in the morning. What I was doing didn't really matter to her. She just sought me out and settled in, right on top of my feet.

She never announced her presence or her intentions. Oftentimes she didn't even say hi or ask me what I was up to. She just sat down. Not beside me or in front of me, but smack dab in the middle of my feet. Even if it meant she had to squeeze between my legs and a counter or wall.

She usually tinkered with a toy she'd brought along. I would hear her talking to herself or maybe singing. To her, this pattern of activity was normal. To me, it was brand-new. Out of all my six children, she was the only one to ever do anything like this. And I treasured every moment. She settled in, content as she could be … until I moved. Because when I moved, that meant she needed to move too.

The twenty-two verses that detail the life of the woman in Proverbs 31 include plenty of things she could have been fearful about. She had a household, business endeavors, and day-to-day projects to keep her occupied—and anxious, if she'd let them.

We too have people and pressures and plans that we bring to God. We talk to God about our children and husbands and even the bed coverings we're making. (Okay, maybe you're not actually making a bed covering, but you know what I mean.) We desire results and ask for blessing, believing that once we receive those things from God, we will smile without fear.

But instead of asking God to secure our futures—or maybe even bringing Him practical, well-thought-out plans that we ask Him to please make happen (politely, of course)—I believe there's a more effective way to gain the security we seek.

You may not be fully convinced that the road to smiling without fear starts with the heart. You may still be wondering how the value God has placed on you through Jesus relates to your fears at all. My goal is that by the end of our time together today, you will have no doubt about the importance of this first step. In order to reach that goal, we're going to take a detour from Proverbs 31, because we need to go all the way back to the beginning.

In the first chapter of the first book of the Bible, we read how God created the world and how He made humans different from the rest of His creation:

> God created man in his own image,
>> in the image of God he created him;
>> male and female he created them. (Gen. 1:27)

Underline the four-word phrase that describes how God created people.

Now, hold on to that thought for a minute, and let's fast-forward to chapter 3: "He [Adam] said, 'I heard the sound of you [God] in the garden, and I was afraid, because I was naked, and I hid myself'" (v. 10).

According to this verse, at what point did Adam become afraid?

What made him afraid?

What did he do because he was afraid?

Here we see two extremes. First, we find creation as God intended it to be. In Genesis 1:27, God created man and woman in His own image. What honor and value God placed on us! Yet just two chapters later, we step into a very different scene.

Genesis 3:10 records the entry of *fear* into our vocabulary. Before this moment, fear did not exist in this way because Adam and Eve lived in perfect union with God. Earlier in Genesis 3, we see Adam and Eve determining in their hearts to disobey God. That was when their relationship with God fractured. This event is referred to as the fall. It is the moment when God's perfect creation became tainted by humankind's sin. From that moment on, everything changed.

Instead of being invited into God's presence, Adam and Eve hid from it.

Instead of having fellowship with God, Adam and Eve were afraid of Him.

Which of these positions best describes your current relationship with God: invited in or hiding and afraid?

The presence of God is the absence of fear. To try to handle fear apart from seeking God's presence is like when I attempted to treat the cracks in my house without repairing the foundation. It doesn't work. Our attempts to arrange a secure future on our own may ease the ache of fear for a moment, but the fear source still remains and will soon show itself again.

If we want to smile without fear, we must first learn to remain in God's presence.

DIGGING IN

Though Adam and Eve's sin brought punishment, God did for them what they could not do for themselves. He covered their shame and provided protection for them as they left the garden of Eden.[1] Though they were banned from returning, they were not banned from God's presence.[2]

Just as God made a way for Adam and Eve to continue to experience His presence in spite of their sin, He has made a way for us to live in His presence.

> I am the vine; you are the branches. If you remain in me and I in you, you will
> bear much fruit; apart from me you can do nothing. (John 15:5 NIV)

What did Jesus call Himself?

What did Jesus call us?

What did He tell us to do?

What did He say would happen if we do?

What did Jesus say we can do apart from Him?

The book of John opens with words that echo Genesis 1: "In the beginning ..." (1:1). Shortly after, John tells us that "the Word became flesh and dwelt among us, and we have seen his glory, glory as of the only Son from the Father, full of grace and truth" (v. 14).

Not only did Jesus leave His rightful place of glory in heaven to enter into His fallen creation, He also explains to us (in John 15) how we can remain in His presence. To *remain* in Jesus is to maintain unbroken fellowship with Him and receive constant influence from Him.[3]

We may not be able to control every detail of the future, but we can live in God's presence and love every day.

Just like my baby girl who sought me out and sat down on my feet. Every time she drew near to me, a couple of things happened. First, she enjoyed fellowship with me. Positioned at my feet, she enjoyed everything I was doing. If I laughed, she could laugh too. If I sang a song, she rocked to the melody. If I was cooking, she inhaled the smells. Being that close to me allowed her access to everything I did. She wouldn't miss a thing.

Second, in my presence she knew she was secure. She could be so confident for a few reasons. For one thing, I could see her. Her actions were exposed in plain sight before me, so she knew that if what she was doing was unhealthy or wrong or unsafe, I would tell her.

For another, she could hear my voice. (Look for more on this next week!) She was close enough to absorb everything I said. Therefore, she was not only sure of her present actions, she was learning for her future too.

Let's read more in John 15. Read verses 1–10 below, and circle or highlight every occurrence of the word *remain*:

> I am the true vine, and my Father is the gardener. He cuts off every branch in me that bears no fruit, while every branch that does bear fruit he prunes so that it will be even more fruitful. You are already clean because of the word I have spoken to you. Remain in me, as I also remain in you. No branch can bear fruit by itself; it must remain in the vine. Neither can you bear fruit unless you remain in me.
>
> I am the vine; you are the branches. If you remain in me and I in you, you will bear much fruit; apart from me you can do nothing. If you do not remain in me, you are like a branch that is thrown away and withers; such branches are picked up, thrown into the fire and burned. If you remain in me and my words remain in you, ask whatever you wish, and it will be done for you. This is to my Father's glory, that you bear much fruit, showing yourselves to be my disciples.
>
> As the Father has loved me, so have I loved you. Now remain in my love. If you keep my commands, you will remain in my love, just as I have kept my Father's commands and remain in his love. (NIV)

In literature, *repetition* is "the repeating of a word or phrase ... to add emphasis and stress."[4] When something is repeated, it is to make sure we don't miss it. In these ten verses, Jesus said "remain" eleven times. Eleven times!

When we remain in Christ, we root ourselves in His presence. When we live rooted in God's presence, fear has no place to grow. And as we remain in Jesus, He transfers the riches of His joy to us. Jesus noted two ways we can remain or abide in Him: we remain in Christ when His words remain in us, and we remain in His love by obeying His commands.

To become women who smile without fear, we must remain in Christ. We may not be able to control every detail of the future, but we can live in God's presence and love every day.

WORK IT OUT

To smile without fear of the future, I need to spend less time *doing* and more time *being* with Jesus.

We are knit together with Christ through the gift of the Holy Spirit. As we stay in God's presence through reading His Word and obeying His commands, we are constantly influenced by Him. When we are constantly influenced by God, we are changed more and more to reflect His image.

I want us to do something to demonstrate this, so find a soft surface. Like for real, right now go and find a soft surface. Maybe you could use the arm of a sofa or chair. Maybe you have some Play-Doh lying around. I'll wait until you find one.

(Insert humming of *Jeopardy!* theme song here.)

Do you have your soft surface? Great. Now hold up three fingers on the same hand. Press those fingers gently into the soft surface, then remove them.

Record what happened:

With a light press and short hold, your fingers likely left an impression on the surface you pressed them into. Your fingers shaped the surface they came in contact with and left a mark that outlined their appearance. And that, sister, is exactly what Jesus Christ will do in our hearts if we remain in Him.

I want you to look back at that soft surface—how does it look now?

There is probably no sign of the impression of your fingers anymore, because you didn't hold them there long enough or push them in deep enough to leave a permanent mark. Therefore, when you removed your fingers, the impression quickly faded.

In order for our hearts to bear the impression of Jesus and produce the fruit we just read about, we have to remain connected to Him, constantly influenced by Him.

> When we live rooted in God's presence,
> fear has no place to grow.

Before we can trust God with our futures, we have to trust Him with our hearts. We have to believe He's done a work for us that we could never do for ourselves, and we have to rest in that alone.

A part of being still each day this week is to allow God to leave His impression on our hearts. But before we do this today, let's consider one thing: the type of surface being impressed. Our impression activity worked only because the surface was soft. If we tried it on a hard surface—a wall or table or book—there would be no impression left behind. A hard surface is not conducive to being impressed.

Today, ask God to create an impressionable heart in you. Then quiet your thoughts, your body, your phone, your television, and anything else that makes noise, and sit with your heart fixed on Jesus.

Use the space below to record any takeaways you have from this time.

_____

_____

_____

_____

_____

_____

We need to get more and more familiar with God's Word.

Day 4

Uninvited Guests

Keep your *heart* with all
diligence / *vigilance* , for from it flow the springs of life.
Proverbs 4:23

The first time we met, it was as if *I* had moved into *his* house. Nestled into my early-morning spot in the living room, I sipped my coffee and enjoyed the silence. The only light was the glow from the Christmas tree in the corner. I thought I was alone … until our houseguest scampered out from under my chair.

He wasn't in a rush. He seemed to be going about his morning chores. He stopped by a stuffed toy on the floor before continuing on toward the fireplace. That's when I shifted in my chair. Something about a mouse crawling around on my floor sparked the urge to tuck my toes underneath my body.

Mr. Mouse heard my shuffle and shuffled himself out of sight. Seconds later, I alerted Luke as if to commission him into a mouse hunt. He did a sweep of the area, then announced that the mouse was long gone, but all day my ears and eyes stayed on high alert.

As I woke my daughters for school the next morning, I saw the shadow. I flipped on the light and woke up anyone still sleeping. Everyone rushed to the girls' room, and sure enough, we identified the shadow as our Christmas mouse houseguest.

For the next half hour, a life-size version of the game Mouse Trap ensued. We eventually scooped him up in a box and introduced him to his new outdoor living arrangements. I slammed the front door and washed my hands. Sure, I still felt a little bit like a mouse might run up my arm, but for the most part, I could laugh at what had just transpired. And the kids weren't even late for school!

The very next morning, our Christmas mouse took up shelter under the Christmas tree skirt. I have a video.

I called Luke on the phone, because at times like this you call a man. He told me to put some food in a box and try to get the mouse to run into it. I said "Absolutely not," so eventually Luke came home and did it. And once again, we escorted Mr. Mouse out the front door to his new home.

Telling this story now, I see the madness of it. Didn't we just set a mouse free the day before? So why in the world did we think this second time would end differently?

On the third day, the mouse didn't wait until the next morning to show himself. No, this time, he waited until everyone in the house went to sleep—or so he thought. Then he climbed up the shelf that sits next to my bed. And in a scene straight out of the movie *Ratatouille*, he stood up on his little hind legs and looked at me as I lay in bed.

Oh, but I wasn't sleeping.

We've been talking all week about our hearts. Hopefully the last three days of study have exposed some places in your heart that needed attention and truth. And while it all can't be summed up in a few days, at least we're off to a good start. Today I want us to turn our attention toward guarding our hearts.

> Keep your heart with all vigilance,
>   for from it flow the springs of life. (Proverbs 4:23)

What does this verse say to do with your heart?

How does it say you should do it?

Why does it say you should do it?

A woman who smiles without fear *keeps* her heart ... relentlessly. The Hebrew word translated "keep" is *natsar* and is used in a variety of ways in Scripture. It can mean "to keep or maintain," "to watch over," and "to defend."[1]

What would you say is your most valuable possession?

How do you treat this possession?

Odds are that once you identified the most valuable thing in your possession, it wasn't hard for you to describe the way you care for it. The things we value become priorities in our lives. They get our full attention. Even when we're not right in front of them, they're on our minds, and we likely allow thoughts of these possessions to distract us from other things. We understand what is at stake, and we take strategic measures to make sure those things we deem most valuable are carefully kept and watched over.

As I consider the things most valuable to me, my children come to mind. When they were little, we would spend time at the lake during the summer months. On those days I spent much of my time on high alert. I counted heads over and over and over again to make sure all six of my children were accounted for. I checked and double-checked life jackets to be sure they were buckled on correctly. At times we lost a towel or a pair of goggles because I didn't keep as close an eye on those things. They weren't nearly as valuable as my boys and girls.

So what about your heart?

When the Christmas mouse took up residence in my house, I took a few wrong steps before I took the right ones. At the first sighting of the mouse, I made a choice to ignore the problem. I knew I'd seen a mouse, and while he did disappear, he disappeared to somewhere. I allowed this transition (to not seeing the mouse) to be enough, and even though my good sense knew that out of sight did not mean gone completely, I chose to ignore it because I couldn't see it.

Sure enough, it was only a matter of time before I saw him again. When I did, I took another wrong step. Instead of eliminating the problem, I merely made more attempts to avoid it. I wanted the mouse out of my house, so I made sure he got out. But I didn't consider things like how he was getting into the house in the first place. I wasn't truly looking to guard my house—I just wanted the problem to go away.

Ignoring and avoiding my problem only prolonged it. Instead of freeing myself, I trapped myself with a faulty solution … until the night my mouse friend wanted to hang out next to my head in my bed.

That was the last straw.

I spent the rest of that night searching things like "how to trap a mouse" on my phone. I did this while sitting in a chair in the middle of the room. (I heard somewhere that mice only travel along a wall because of poor eyesight. If it's not true, don't tell me!) First thing the next morning, I called the pest control.

Later that day, the exterminator arrived with a wealth of knowledge about our uninvited houseguests. That's right—I used the plural form of the word. Apparently, we had a whole group of mice feasting on the crumbs in our house. The exterminator found where they were getting inside and knew just what to use to deter them from coming in again. Oh, and I also brought a cat home. I leaned on what I knew to be true from the old cartoon *Tom and Jerry*: mice don't like cats. One cat = zero mice. There's another math problem for you.

We've never seen a mouse in the house again.

Just as I had to finally get serious about removing the mouse from my house, if we want to smile without fear, we have to get serious about keeping our hearts.

DIGGING IN

Look up and read 1 Peter 5:6–8.

What is the name of the enemy of your heart? (v. 8)

The devil

What four steps can you take to resist him? (vv. 6–8)

Humble yourselves
Cast your anxiety on Him
Be alert
and of sober mind

The pest that torments your heart has a name, and he's not a little field mouse scurrying around the house, looking for a place to hide. The Bible compares him to a lion seeking you with the intention to devour you. This isn't something we can afford to ignore or try to avoid. To resist the Devil, we need a plan. God has given us His Word to help us be proactive in standing against our enemy. The Devil will attack us daily with lies, temptations, distractions, and fear, and we need to be ready to resist him.

Pause for a minute to consider: Is there anything in your life that you know you need to deal with that you are ignoring or avoiding instead of proactively resisting the Devil?

Of the four steps you listed on the previous page, are some more difficult than the others? Which ones? Why do you think they're more difficult?

The NIV translation of Proverbs 4:23 uses these words: "Above all else, guard your heart." This whole week's study is titled "There's a Heart behind This" because "from [the heart] flow the springs of life." If we want to be women who smile without fear, we have to be women who keep our hearts diligently. We can't take this lightly.

Let's look at a few strategies we can employ to help us keep vigilant watch over our hearts and resist the Devil.

Replace lies with truth. We need to answer the lies the Devil feeds us with the truth. Truth isn't what your friend told you or even what your mama said—truth is the infallible Word of God. We need to get more and more familiar with God's Word. We need to know it and use it as we seek to relentlessly keep our hearts.

As this point relates to our fears, sometimes we actually can talk ourselves into believing it's necessary to fear the future. We can convince ourselves that worrying about the future will somehow make us better prepared for it. But that's not what Jesus said! God's Word is full of verses that tell us not to fear. At the end of this week, I've included a resource called "Keep Your Heart" that includes ten truths from God's Word to help you with this. Look at these, memorize them, and pray them.

Be thankful. Gratitude turns our thoughts away from our concerns and onto God's goodness. The book of Psalms is full of songs of praise and thanksgiving to God. You can find a list of thanksgiving psalms in the "Keep Your Heart" resource. Use these as a starting line to help you foster a heart of gratitude.

Search your heart often. Sin is one of the Devil's greatest tools to trap us and trip us up. If he can get us to trade the truth of God for a lie and engage in a sinful pattern of life, then we're set on a path of destruction. In order to keep our hearts healthy, we need to do heart checkups regularly. Just as an annual visit to your doctor tells you about the physical health of your heart, a heart checkup helps you evaluate the spiritual health of your heart and prevent potential problems. In the "Keep Your Heart" resource, I've included a prayer to guide you through a heart checkup. You can use this prayer or write one of your own.

WORK IT OUT

> ✎ To smile without fear of the future, I need to spend less time *doing* and more time *being* with Jesus. ✎

Go back to the "Digging In" section, and consider the list of things you may be trying to ignore or avoid. In what ways is the Devil keeping you trapped by these things?

Remember, the Devil is portrayed as a lion on the prowl—hunting, hiding, slinking so as not to be seen until it's too late and he has his prey locked in his jaws. Really consider this, and ask God to fully reveal it to you. Your enemy could be using a favorite song that whispers lies, a cell phone that fuels distraction, a habit that indulges sin, or a television show that breeds fear. Then quiet your thoughts, your body, your phone, your television, and anything else that makes noise, and sit with your heart fixed on Jesus.

Use the space below to record what God reveals.

_____

_____

_____

_____

_____

_____

_____

_____

_____

_____

We need to get more and more familiar with God's Word.

Day 5

A Woman of Noble Character

Memory Verse

Guard your *heart* with all *vigilance*,
for from it flow the springs *of* life.

Proverbs 4:23

Spending so much time with this woman who smiles without fear brought up a question in my heart. An uncomfortable question but an important one.

I've been hanging out pretty regularly with this woman for several years, and in that time, I've encountered days that don't bring up a smile in my heart. My family has faced injury, hardship, and death. We've walked through sickness and sadness, hurt and deep disappointment. With friends we've walked through similar things.

And that's just in my own small world. When I look around at the desperate—so desperate—circumstances across the globe, I've had to ask God the very honest question: *Is this really for every woman? Could every woman in every circumstance actually be a woman who smiles without fear of the future?*

That's when God reminded me of Ruth. You may know her too.

She's the only named woman in the Bible who is described as a woman of noble character (Ruth 3:11 NIV)—the same phrase used to describe the Proverbs 31 woman. Ruth is a real-life example of what this woman looks like and how she smiles without fear. Ruth's life confirms the truth that any woman in any circumstance can be a woman of noble character who smiles without fear.

Open your Bible, and read the first chapter of the book of Ruth.

We meet Ruth and two other widows on a road lined with death and poverty. Orpah and Ruth, both Moabites, had married sons of Naomi, an Israelite living in their country. With her husband and sons dead, Naomi knew she could not provide for her daughters-in-law. Her future looked bleak, so she departed for her homeland and begged them to stay in Moab, where they could remarry and be cared for.

Ruth 1:14–15 tells us what Orpah and Ruth decided.

What did Orpah do?

She went back

What did Ruth do?

She stayed with Naomi

According to Ruth 1:16, why did Ruth go with Naomi?

Where you go I will go

Despite how hopeless the situation seemed, Ruth decided to trust God on that road. Chapters 2–3 of the book of Ruth detail her determination to be faithful with each day in a new land. We see her set out to glean in the fields behind the harvesters—taking advantage of a provision God had made in the Law to care for the poor people of Israel (see Lev. 19:9–10). We read about how Ruth cared for Naomi and supported her. And as we watch her story of faithfulness unfold, we see God do something only He could orchestrate.

In her faithfulness to serve God and others, Ruth went to work in a field belonging to a man named Boaz, a relative of Naomi. Boaz took notice of Ruth, and being legally able to marry her, he did so. Ruth gave birth to a son they named Obed—a man whom God included in the lineage of His own Son, Jesus (see Matt. 1:5).

When we dance to the rhythm of daily faithfulness, as Ruth did, God can turn our situational prisons into supernatural positions. And though we might not actually laugh out loud and frolic through every day, we can live with an inner stability that is not defeated or shaken by life's storms.

WORK IT OUT

To smile without fear of the future, I need to spend less time *doing* and more time *being* with Jesus.

Use the space below to share your heart with God. What things have you struggled with this week? What things have brought you hope and a breath of fresh air? What questions or concerns are you wrestling with? Are you confused about anything? What burden keeps coming up in your heart?

Before you write, here are a few suggestions to help you on day 5 of each week:

- Be honest. God knows your thoughts already. There's no need to try to make them sound pretty or how you think they should sound. Start with honesty.
- Don't try to make complete sentences or punctuate accurately. This isn't a test. No one will be proofreading it or asking you what you meant. This is between you and God, and He knows what you mean.
- Don't give yourself a word-count goal or force words that aren't there. Sometimes one word is all you need. At other times the space I leave you won't be enough.
- Don't feel like you have to do it all at one time. Take this book with you. Put it in your purse or car, and pull it out throughout the day—or over the course of several days—and continue this conversation with God.

- Show up. Even if you're busy. Even if you're hurting. Even if you feel like you have nothing to say. Keep trusting that when you show up, God will meet you.

I pray this week has been refreshing for you, and I hope, as we head into the coming weeks, you feel prepared with a heart conditioned to respond to God.

Keep Your Heart

Replace Lies with Truth: Ten Promises from God's Word

1. "God gave us a spirit not of fear but of power and love and self-control" (2 Tim. 1:7).

2. "Do not fear, for I am with you; do not be dismayed, for I am your God. I will strengthen you and help you; I will uphold you with my righteous right hand" (Isa. 41:10 NIV).

3. "You are from God, little children, and have overcome them; because greater is He who is in you than he who is in the world" (1 John 4:4 NASB).

4. "Do not fret *or* have any anxiety about anything, but in every circumstance *and* in everything, by prayer and petition (definite requests), *with* thanksgiving, continue to make your wants known to God. And God's peace … which transcends all understanding shall garrison *and* mount guard over your hearts and minds in Christ Jesus" (Phil. 4:6–7 AMPC).

5. "Some trust in chariots and some in horses, but we trust in the name of the LORD our God" (Ps. 20:7).

6. "You have not received a spirit that makes you fearful slaves. Instead, you received God's Spirit when he adopted you as his own children. Now we call him, 'Abba, Father'" (Rom. 8:15 NLT).

7. "Casting the whole of your care [all your anxieties, all your worries, all your concerns, once and for all] on Him, for He cares for you affectionately *and* cares about you watchfully" (1 Pet. 5:7 AMPC).

8. "God is our Refuge and Strength [mighty *and* impenetrable to temptation], a very present *and* well-proved help in trouble" (Ps. 46:1 AMPC).

9. "I know how to live on almost nothing or with everything. I have learned the secret of living in every situation, whether it is with a full stomach or empty, with plenty or little. For I can do everything through Christ, who gives me strength" (Phil. 4:12–13 NLT).

10. "Who of you by worrying can add a single hour to your life?… And do not set your heart on what you will eat or drink; do not worry about it…. But seek his kingdom, and these things will be given to you as well" (Luke 12:25, 29, 31 NIV).

Be Thankful: Eight Psalms of Thanksgiving to Get You Started

1. Psalm 30
2. Psalm 33
3. Psalm 34
4. Psalm 65
5. Psalm 75
6. Psalm 107
7. Psalm 116
8. Psalm 118

Search Your Heart: A Prayer for a Heart Checkup

Lord, explore my heart and point out anything in me that offends You. Break my heart for the things in my life that break Your heart. When You do, may I be quick to respond. Expose the quiet notions that cross my mind daily that are indicators of hidden sin in my heart. I want to get serious about my sin. Help me take inventory of my thoughts and make them obedient to You. Shed light on any lies, and help me replace them with truth. Uncover any lusts of the flesh, and strengthen me as I commit to fleeing from them. In Jesus' name, amen.

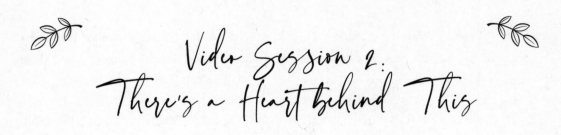

Video Session 2:
There's a Heart behind This

Watch video session 2, and use this space to write notes or record insights.

_____
_____
_____
_____
_____
_____
_____
_____
_____
_____
_____
_____
_____
_____
_____
_____
_____
_____
_____
_____
_____

Week 2

Her Heart's Position: Living Secure

✿

Memory Verse

*You did not receive the spirit of slavery to fall back
into fear, but you have received the Spirit of adoption
as sons, by whom we cry, "Abba! Father!"*

Romans 8:15

Introduction

"Dad, I'm scared!"

I knew that voice. I didn't need binoculars to confirm it. My oldest son needed help, and I wanted to save him. But all I could do was watch.

Just a few hours earlier, as we had traveled our well-worn path of animal observation at the local zoo, we had stumbled upon something new. Out of nowhere, a fresh attraction had popped up. We approached the straw-covered hut and discovered a ropes course. And a sea of hands raised as our kids volunteered to go first.

Our littlest two weren't yet tall enough for the adventure, so while Luke escorted four eager kids down the path to the ropes course, I took the younger ones for a bathroom break. A few minutes later, we wove down the tree-lined path and stepped into a clearing, where I found my four oldest children dangling four stories above the ground.

My heart fluttered a bit. I'm not sure what I expected when I heard the words *ropes course*, but this wasn't it. Yes, they were all decked out in helmets and safety gear. Yes, they were strapped into harnesses that kept them from plummeting to the ground. But my mama heart was still quite uncomfortable with my kids playing near the clouds.

As I tried to pretend to be okay, I knelt down next to my children still safely on the ground and coached them to wave at those dots up in the sky. "Yes," I assured them, "those dots are your brothers and sister."

It was then that I heard the heart-piercing cry of my son Jonah: "Dad, I'm scared!"

He had gotten away from the others. He'd set off on his own, but before long he'd realized just how far below his feet the safe ground was. He couldn't take one more step across the wobbly planks. Fear had seized him, and there he stood, gripping a rope in each hand. Frozen in fear.

From the other side of what felt like a cavern of air separating us, I tried to answer Jonah's call, but I knew my attempts to help were futile. I was all the way down on the ground. I saw him and I heard him—but only from a distance. Even if Jonah could hear my voice, he likely wouldn't be able to understand my words. I could only watch as the scene unfolded.

That's when I heard the calm, assuring voice of Jonah's father. "Jonah, I see you and I'm right here with you."

Luke's words didn't stop my son's body from quivering, but his voice did silence Jonah's cry for help.

"I'm going to help you," Luke said. "Just do what I say. The first thing you need to do is let go of the rope with your right hand and grab the one in front of you."

And Jonah did.

"Great job, son. You're doing great. Now take your right foot, and move it onto the step in front of you."

And Jonah did.

"All right, good, Jonah. You're doing good. Now you're going to have to let go with your left hand and reach out for the rope ahead. I know it's scary, Jonah. But you can do it."

And Jonah did.

His dad continued to give gentle, patient, step-by-step instructions, and Jonah continued to follow them. One step at a time, a father guided his son to safety.

Day 1

The Definition of Security

Memory Verse

You did not receive the spirit of slavery to fall back into fear, but you have received the Spirit of adoption as sons, by whom we cry, "Abba! Father!"

Romans 8:15

Sometimes I think we treat *fear* like it's a bad word. Like one of those words we spell out rather than say. Somehow we've come to believe that when we are afraid, we'd better keep it to ourselves and find a way to deal with it. But when we treat our fears this way, they don't disappear. Instead, all we've done is stuff them down into our hearts. And stuffing our fears only gives them room to grow.

It's like packing a suitcase. I'm an expert at this because I hate to check a bag at the airport. Instead, I try to carry everything for my trip in two bags—one small enough to fit in the overhead bin and another small enough to go under the seat in front of me. I roll things up and jam them into little, unknown crevices. I wedge things down the walls of the bag. I arrange my clothes in a way that leaves room for more. I have successfully made five-day trips like this. I'm a great stuffer.

Just as I stuff clothes into my bag, we can stuff fears into our hearts. We push them down, squeezing them into hidden places. We attempt to play the "out of sight, out of mind" game. But to no avail. Because we haven't actually *answered* our fears … we've only made room for more.

On the ropes course, Jonah made a brave decision to cry out to his father. He acknowledged his fear and looked to his dad for help.

Possibly the most important decision any of us could ever make when we face our fears is to cry out to our Father for rescue.

Where do you instinctively turn when you're afraid? You might turn to a friend or family member, a habit or hobby, or maybe even a website that helps you gather information and make a plan. Use the space below to write down the places or people you turn to when you're scared.

Now consider how you feel after you've turned to these places or people. Do you finish your conversations with peace? Do you walk away from the computer or food or television show with rest in your soul?

Some of us have hearts packed with fears we've never released. We've never cried out for rescue, and any minute now, the zipper holding all these fears inside will burst and spill our infected souls onto the people and places around us.

You might even believe you're the only one who faces fears. You look around at the women in your life, or even at this woman in Proverbs 31, and you might think they're never afraid, at least not like you are. But I'm convinced that the woman in Proverbs 31 doesn't smile without fear of the future because she never fears the future.

Read Proverbs 31:20, 27–28, and list some of the people she cares for.

the poor and needy
her children
her husband

Read Proverbs 31:15, 19, 21, 23, and list some of the pressures she encounters.

Not enough time.
making warm, suitable clothes for her family

Read Proverbs 31:16–18, and list some of the plans she invests in.

a field, a vineyard

I think we can all agree that this woman has plenty to fear. If she smiles without fear of the future, it's not because she never fears the future. She smiles because she knows where to turn when she does.

DIGGING IN

Read Romans 8:15:

> You did not receive the spirit of slavery to fall back into fear, but you have received the Spirit of adoption as sons, by whom we cry, "Abba! Father!"

This verse details two different spirits with two very different outcomes. We can live as slaves, or we can live as sons. Use the space below to describe what comes to mind when you read the word *slaves*.

someone with no power, cannot get free from bondage to another

Now record what comes to mind when you read the word *sons*.

lives freely in the care of another

I pray you've only heard about slavery. However, based on statistics and the realities of modern history, I know it is possible that you may have experienced slavery yourself or have a heritage that knows all too well the horrors of human slavery. Whether slavery has come close to your reality or not, I imagine the contrast between slaves and sons is an easy one to identify.

In the book of Romans, Paul was writing to the Christians in the city of Rome. One of his goals was to assure them of their security as believers in Jesus, both for this life and for eternity.

As followers of Jesus, God has given us His Spirit and welcomed us into His family. He invites us to call on Him as a loving Father. The very next verse in Romans 8 confirms we *are* His children: "The Spirit himself bears witness with our spirit that we are children of God" (v. 16).

> *Possibly the most important decision any of us could ever make when we face our fears is to cry out to our Father for rescue.*

The question becomes, *Do we live like it?* When we choose not to cry out to God—when we try to hide our fears or turn to anything else besides God for help—it's as though we refuse this gift we have received through Jesus. I call this a spiritual stiff-arm.

What keeps you from crying out to God?

For some, the choice not to cry out to God could be due to our definition of *security*. We desire lives that are untouched by suffering and free from struggle. The truth is that this kind of security is not promised. As we continue reading in Romans 8, our security is actually linked to sure suffering:

If [we are] children, then [we are also] heirs—heirs of God and fellow heirs with Christ, provided we suffer with him in order that we may also be glorified with him. (v. 17)

I know this isn't making you feel very secure. It's possibly feeling quite the opposite. But hang in there with me, and let's go back up on the ropes course for a minute and talk about what did *not* happen.

When Luke heard his son's cry for help, Luke did *not* turn into an American Ninja Warrior on the ropes course. He did *not* suspend himself on the ropes like a monkey on forest vines. Luke did *not* swoop in, sweep Jonah up, and swing him to the safety of the next platform. While that would have been awesome, that's not what Luke did.

Could he have done it? Maybe. He was a professional athlete, after all. Could God do that in our lives when we face a future that feels scary? Absolutely. But He doesn't always work that way.

It would be so much nicer to think that when we make the brave choice to cry out, "God, I'm scared," we could count on Him to swoop in and swing us straight to safety. And sometimes He does! But I'm finding that a lot of times God chooses to guide me one step at a time. Instead of rescuing us immediately, He assures us with His calm, steady voice, *"I see you, and I'm here with you."* Then, with gentleness and patience, encouraging us all the way, God leads us step by step until we reach a safe place.

When he followed his dad's voice one step at a time, Jonah arrived at a much larger and sturdier platform. He breathed a big sigh of relief and even smiled a little as he looked back at what he and his dad had conquered together. Then Jonah turned to face the rest of the course, and without a hint of hesitation, he continued. It seemed pretty simple now.

Here's the thing. I wonder if the rest of the ropes course would have been so easy for Jonah if Luke had chosen the sweep, swoop, and swing method instead of guiding him one step at a time. I don't think it would have been. In fact, I wonder if Jonah would have continued at all.

As Luke guided Jonah through the ropes course in spite of his fear, Jonah grew more confident with every step. More confident in his dad's instruction. More confident in his ability to follow his dad. And most of all, more confident that if his dad said he could do it, then he could do it.

In all these things we are more than conquerors through him who loved us. For I am sure that neither death nor life, nor angels nor rulers, nor things present nor things to come, nor powers, nor height nor depth, nor anything else in all creation, will be able to separate us from the love of God in Christ Jesus our Lord. (Rom. 8:37–39)

Circle the words *these things* above. Go back and read verse 35. List some of the things Paul was talking about.

trouble, hardship, famine, Persecution

We can seek security by trying to orchestrate all the details of our lives, or we can rest assured that, no matter what we face, God is for us, God is good, and nothing can separate us from His love. Nothing—absolutely nothing—can separate us from our Father. No matter what we face, we can always cry, "Abba! Father!" Whether it's a cry of celebration or desperation, we always have a place to go.

WORK IT OUT

God can handle every one of your doubts and fears. Not only *can* He handle them but He also *wants* to handle them. God invites you to call on Him at any time for any reason.

Take some time today to admit your fears to God. Whatever fear has been caked into the crevices of your heart for too long, today is the day to let it go. I encourage you to be specific. Your cry invites the guidance of His voice, which I'm excited to talk more with you about this week. For now you can start with these words: "God, I'm scared!"

Use the space below to write out your prayer or record what God reveals to you.

_____

_____

_____

Nothing —absolutely nothing —can
separate us from our Father.

Day 2

The Great Exchange

Memory Verse

You did not receive the spirit of _____ to

fall back into _____, but you have received the Spirit

of adoption as sons, by whom we cry, "Abba! Father!"

Romans 8:15

I had never experienced darkness like this.

I had heard about it—a darkness so thick that you couldn't even make out your hand if you held it in front of your face. And since this seemed to be *that* kind of darkness, I tested it. I raised my hand and placed it inches in front of my eyes. Sure enough, I couldn't see it. I couldn't even make out the outline of my fingers.

Moments before, I had stood in a well-lit hallway just outside my boys' bedroom. As our bedtime routine came to a close, I moved from room to room to say prayers and give good-night hugs. My boys were already snuggled in their beds as I approached their room. I had expected the lights to be turned off and the room to be dark, but I hadn't expected this.

Though I stood in a familiar place doing a familiar thing, that kind of darkness startled me. My heart rate sped up and a clammy feeling engulfed me. I stood still for a moment to gather myself. After a deep breath and a little pep talk, I continued on the mission I had set out to accomplish—bedtime, of course.

As I moved, something surprising happened. What once was thick, debilitating darkness became maneuverable. I couldn't see well. I'm pretty sure I still stubbed my toe on a toy train or Lego, but I could see. My eyes had adjusted. Slowly, not surely, I inched around the dark room and prayed with my boys.

And the longer I stayed, the more comfortable I grew in the darkness that had once blinded me.

The image of this woman who smiles without fear is one that expresses freedom. The Hebrew word translated "smiles" in Proverbs 31:25 (NASB) has also been translated "frolic."[1] When I hear that word I can't help but think of a little girl in pigtails skipping through a flowery meadow. She's carefree and confident. Nothing weighs her down. With a smile on her face and a giggle in her heart, she laughs.

Can you think of the last time you frolicked? Something about growing up makes us trade the freedom of frolicking for a fear of the future.

Maybe we become more aware. Maybe we become more responsible. Or maybe we have an experience much like mine when I stepped out of the light and into the dark room. Something happens that shocks us into such darkness that we feel lost and blinded. We're consumed by our situation and paralyzed by what we've experienced.

But the longer we live in it, the more adjusted we become. We inch our way around and grow more and more familiar with this new normal. Eventually we forget that there ever was a day when we walked in the light. We don't look for it anymore. We don't long for it. We simply manage in this altered state.

The woman in Proverbs 31 isn't unaware or irresponsible. As we discovered yesterday, pressures and threats pierce her everyday life too. Yet she is described as a woman who smiles at the future. And while we aren't given details of her past, present, or future, there is one verse that tells us all we need to know about how she can smile without fear of the future: "Charm is deceitful, and beauty is vain, but a woman who fears the LORD is to be praised" (v. 30).

The woman in Proverbs 31 is a woman who fears the LORD. She exchanges the fear of the future for the fear of the LORD. And if we want to smile without fear, we too need to make this swap.

Which brings us to our second step toward smiling without fear:

> ✼ **To smile without fear of the future, I need to exchange the** *fear of the future* **for the** *fear of the LORD.* ✼

You may read "the fear of the LORD" and feel like this is a deep concept too big for you to understand. I would agree with you that, yes, this is a deep concept that we may never understand in its entirety. But it is not out of reach to comprehend it in such a way that we can use it and choose it. In fact, I think it's so vital to our lives that we can't afford not to try.

Or you may hear "the fear of the LORD" and be completely discouraged. Because you know all too well what fear can do to your life—so why would you want more of it? Fear has trapped you and oppressed you for far too long. You picked up this study hoping for a solution, and this doesn't feel like one. To attach the word *fear* to *the LORD* is more than just disappointing—it's defeating. But let me assure you that this fear, the fear of the LORD, is nothing like the fear of the future.

Draw a line to match each Scripture below with what it says about the fear of the LORD.

Psalm 34:7	helps us act rightly toward one another
Proverbs 14:26	is always for our good
Proverbs 19:23	invites God's protection and deliverance
Deuteronomy 6:24	creates confidence for today and the future
Leviticus 25:17	leads to life and rest

How do these verses change your thoughts on the fear of the LORD?

As a woman who fears the LORD, the Proverbs 31 woman submits her life to God and finds assurance in His authority. She worships Him, rests in Him, and places security in Him alone. To become women who smile without fear of the future, we must first become women who fear the LORD.

DIGGING IN

The verses we just read help us form a better understanding of what we stand to gain when we exchange the fear of the future for the fear the LORD, but we still need to answer how exactly we accomplish it. What does it mean to fear the LORD?

To answer this question, let's read a few verses from Deuteronomy:

> Now, Israel, what does the LORD your God require of you, but to fear the LORD your God, to walk in all his ways, to love him, to serve the LORD your God with all your heart and with all your soul, and to keep the commandments and statutes of the LORD, which I am commanding you today for your good? (10:12–13)

Based on these verses, list four ways we can practice living in the fear of the LORD:

In Deuteronomy, the nation of Israel stood poised to possess the land God had promised to them. Moses, the man appointed by God to lead the nation out of slavery in Egypt, recounted what God had done to bring them to this place and reminded them how to remain in unbroken fellowship with Him. So much is packed into these four ways to live out the fear of the LORD. Let's dig into them.

To smile without fear of the future, I need to exchange the fear of the future for the fear of the Lord.

First, God tells us to *walk in all His ways*. The idea of walking in God's ways implies regularity. In Old Testament times people walked more than we do today. It was their primary form of transportation. When Moses delivered this message from the Lord to the nation of Israel, they had just walked with God through the wilderness. The instruction to *walk* in all of God's ways means we are to do it consistently—every day in every way.

Second, we're instructed to *love God*. The word *love* is thrown around in our world today so much that it can be hard to truly understand what it means. The Hebrew word translated "love" in this verse is *'ahab*, which is defined as "to desire, to breathe after."[2] The Bible tells us that real love is not our love for God but His love for us—shown by sending Jesus as a sacrifice for our sins (see 1 John 4:10). God is love and is our perfect example of love. The outward expression of our love for God is to walk in His ways and keep His commandments. Basically, the other three things on this list happen if we love God.

Third, you practice the fear of the LORD as you *serve God with all your heart and all your soul*. In Matthew 6:24 Jesus said, "No one can serve two masters." He elaborated with distinct contrasts, saying, "Either he will hate the one and love the other, or he will be devoted to the one and despise the other. You cannot serve God and money." The Amplified Bible notes that the Greek word for "money" can extend to "possessions, fame, status, or whatever is valued more than the Lord" (AMP). Who we serve proves who or what we love.

And finally, God tells us to *keep His commandments*. The definition of the word translated "keep" in this verse is not all that different from the word in last week's verse that instructed us to "keep" our hearts (Prov. 4:23). It carries the idea of guarding and observing God's commandments the same way we would care for a garden. This is not the picture of a halfhearted attempt to do right. Instead, it urges us to place God's Word as a priority in our lives and to constantly keep it before our eyes and our hearts so that we are careful to obey all that is written in it.

Walk, love, serve, keep … which of these is easiest for you? Which one is most difficult?

I know this is getting deep. So if you need to, consider this a thirty-second time-out. Stand up, go get a glass of water, look out the window for a minute, and come back. Because there's one more thing I don't want us to miss about the fear of the LORD.

At its core, the fear of the LORD is an expression of worship. It is a deep awe of who God is. The fear of the LORD lives in our hearts when we are so humbled by God's holiness that our natural response is to give Him our whole lives.

> I appeal to you therefore, brothers, by the mercies of God, to present your bodies as a living sacrifice, holy and acceptable to God, which is your spiritual worship. (Rom. 12:1)

Just as we read yesterday in Romans 8, Paul had been sharing with the Roman Christians the riches and wisdom of God. In light of that, Paul urged his readers to offer themselves as a living sacrifice to God. The ESV calls this action your *spiritual* worship. Other translations use words like *reasonable* or *rational* (KJV, AMP).

When we see God as He truly is, we will see ourselves as we truly are and will have no other option but to fall at His feet and present ourselves as a living sacrifice. In week 1, we learned to remain in Christ. This week, we will learn to revere Him.

Maybe you feel that sense of awe today, and maybe you don't. Either way, I hope you begin to crave it more and more. As we move through this week of study, I hope you experience it more and more. No matter where you are with this, you can always cry out to God and ask, "Help me love You more. Help me know You more. Give me an awe for who You are."

WORK IT OUT

> ✺ To smile without fear of the future, I need to exchange the *fear of the future* for the *fear of the LORD*. ✺

Look at the following chart, and consider each exchange that takes place when we exchange the fear of the future for the fear of the LORD. Ask God to show you some examples in your own life, and add them in the empty boxes.

FEAR OF THE FUTURE ...	FEAR OF THE LORD ...
says I am in charge	says God is in charge
focuses on the problem	focuses on who God is
forces me to feel prepared for anything	trusts God to give me what I need when I need it
lives distracted by the future	lives faithful today
clings and controls	releases and rests

Go back to the matching exercise in today's study, and review the rewards of the fear of the LORD. What might be different in your life if you exchanged the fear of the future for the fear of the LORD? Use the space below to record your thoughts.

When we see God as He truly is, we will see ourselves as we truly are and will have no other option but to fall at His feet and present ourselves as a living sacrifice.

Day 3

Do You Know or Do You Know?

Memory Verse

You did not receive the spirit of ___*fear*___ *to fall back into* ___*slavery*___ *, but you have received the Spirit of* ___*adoption*___ *as sons, by whom we cry, "Abba! Father!"*

Romans 8:15

I know her.

I've seen her kitchen and her front porch. I know the names of her kids and where she works. I know where she went to college, and I even know some of her childhood struggles. I'm pretty sure I know the paint color she used in her daughter's bedroom and that she loves plants. Loves them.

My kids even know who she is, and they ask me from time to time to invite her to our house (usually when there's a decorating emergency).

Yes, Joanna Gaines could totally be my friend.

I've read about her and listened to her. I've smiled at the pictures she shares on social media. I know so much about her. If I bumped into Joanna at a restaurant, I feel sure I would recognize her.

You might too. You've probably at least heard of her. She and her husband have made headlines for several years with a popular show on HGTV that turned into books, a magazine, and a restaurant.

There's just one problem—I've never actually met her.

All of what I know about Joanna Gaines is informational. It's subject matter filtered through media outlets that allow me glimpses into her life and what she's like, but it is nowhere close to the real thing. No matter how much I think I know about her, we're not friends. I don't call her when I need something. I don't share my heart with her. In reality, we are in no way connected.

And I'm afraid, if we're not careful, our relationship with God can look like this too.

There's a lot of information available to us about God these days. We can learn about Him on our computers, on our phones, in church buildings, or in bookstores. In a lot of places on earth, information about God is at our fingertips. Because of this, we can get the impression that we know Him.

But if we're not careful, our connection to God can become the accumulation of information only, void of any relationship.

Read Proverbs 31:30 again: "Charm is deceitful, and beauty is vain, but a woman who fears the LORD is to be praised."

Go back and read Proverbs 31:10–31. Based on our discussion of the fear of the LORD yesterday, look for the characteristics of the fear of the LORD in the actions of the Proverbs 31 woman. In the blanks below, write some examples of how her actions demonstrate the fear of the LORD.

Walk in all His ways	can laugh @ the days to come
Love God	
Serve God with all your heart and soul	opens heart to the poor
Keep His commandments	

Even broken down into these four pieces, this is still a lot to chew on. So I want to draw a starting line for us. To fear the LORD, we have to know God. To walk in all His ways, to keep His commands, to love God and serve Him with all our hearts, we must first know Him.

DIGGING IN

A few different Greek words are translated "know" in the New Testament. One word, *oida*, is primarily defined as "to know a fact."[1] The other word, *ginōskō*, describes knowledge based on personal experience. Let's look at a verse in Scripture to get a better idea of what I'm talking about:

> We *know* that the Son of God has come and has given us understanding, so
> that we may *know* him who is true; and we are in him who is true, in his Son
> Jesus Christ. He is the true God and eternal life. (1 John 5:20)

In this verse, these two Greek words for "know" are used. The one used first—"We *know* that the Son of God has come and has given us understanding"—is *oida*. This is fact-based knowledge that Jesus, the Son of God, came into the world. John wasn't sharing something with his readers for the first time. Instead, he was appealing to their understanding of an experience already stored in their minds. This wasn't news to them.

Based on this definition, what are some things you know about God? List them here.

It's interesting to me that John started with *oida*. Informational knowledge isn't a bad thing, but as it relates to God it can't be the only thing.

The second *know*—"so that we may *know* him who is true"—involves more than the mind. This is a *ginōskō* knowing.

The verse describes a shift where what we know in our minds transfers to our hearts. This is the difference between knowing about people and actually knowing them. Not to get too PG-13, but Jewish people might use this word to describe the way a man and woman would "know" each other on their wedding night.[2] Relational, not informational.

I love how the Amplified Bible translates this portion of 1 John 5:20: "so that we may [progressively and personally] know Him who is true" (AMP).

I want to *progressively and personally* know Jesus.

I know a lot about Joanna Gaines, but I am not progressively getting to know her more personally every day. My knowledge of her is purely informational and will probably always remain so. There's no relationship … and that's okay. But I don't want my knowledge of God to be this way.

There has to be a point at which what we know about God in our minds becomes real in our hearts. We have to come to a moment when all the information we possess *about* God transfers to the desire for a progressive, personal relationship *with* God through Jesus Christ. When knowing in the mind becomes knowing in the heart. Because to know God—to recognize His voice beyond a shadow of a doubt and to trust His choices—we can't just know about Him. We have to live in relationship with Him, progressively and personally.

We have to come to a moment when all the information we possess about God transfers to the desire for a progressive, personal relationship with God through Jesus Christ.

The entire time that my son Jonah tackled his fears on the ropes course, his dad stood behind him. When Jonah cried out for help, he couldn't see Luke. When Luke answered Jonah, Jonah only heard his voice. Yet Jonah knew beyond a shadow of a doubt whose voice he was following.

I know this because, had Jonah for one second believed it was his brother doing the talking, I doubt he would have been so quick to listen. Even if Jonah thought he heard the course instructor's voice, I'm not so sure he would have gone. After all, he had met the instructor only a few minutes earlier. The certainty of knowing that it was his father's voice guiding him gave Jonah the courage to follow in spite of the fears swirling around him.

How could he be so sure it was Luke's voice?

Because he spends time with his dad.

In his very first minutes on this earth, that voice read the Bible to him. Every morning, that voice asks him whether he's brushed his teeth and made his bed. That voice corrects him when he's testing the boundaries of respect and obedience. His dad's voice teaches him new things and encourages him as he learns. That unmistakable voice is one Jonah has heard every day for more than a decade.

You probably know some voices that well too. Think about the voices you hear on phone calls. I know we have caller ID these days, but for a minute imagine you lived in a world without caller ID. There are likely some voices you could identify by simply hearing them say "Hello."

My twin sister's voice is one of those for me. All she says is "Hey," and I know it's her. She doesn't announce herself on the phone call. She knows I know her voice because we've spent so much of life talking to each other.

If we want to know God's voice, we have to spend time with Him.

How do you spend time with God?

I know, I know—it sounds simple enough. But the truth is that spending time with God—reading the Bible, praying, and listening for His voice—can feel overwhelming. The Bible is a pretty good-sized book, and some chapters can definitely be head-scratchers. There you are, resolved to get into God's Word so you can know His voice and trust His choices. You close your eyes, spin around, open the Bible, and point to the page, believing this is the chapter from which God wants to teach you great and mighty things. And inevitably you land in Leviticus … in the chapter about skin disease. Hmm.

But don't get discouraged! Because, in the same way you don't have to tackle your fears alone, you don't have to read the Bible alone either. I've included at the end of this week an assessment to help you find the best option for spending time with God. In the meantime, let's get practical about how this looks in everyday life.

First, as we seek out God's voice, we have to be intentional about hearing it. Life can be noisy. Almost every place we go, there's an opportunity to hear some kind of sound. A podcast or the radio while we drive. The television or YouTube at home. Background music in the elevator. People's voices at work or in a restaurant. Our hearts and minds are bombarded daily with sound.

But think about the last time you had an important face-to-face conversation. How did you handle it? You probably predetermined a day and time so you could clear your schedule of interruptions and distractions. You likely sought out a quiet place—like a coffee shop instead of a football game. You may have even turned off your cell phone to have this talk. Now we're talking crazy, I know.

Second, to grow progressively and personally in our relationship with God, we need to treat our time with Him as a priority. Yes, we can get it in when it fits in. And sometimes that's our best option. But to truly know God in a life-changing way, we may have to fight for time with Him.

To become women who smile without fear, we have to know God. And to do that, we have to spend time with our Father. Our goal should be to spend so much time with God that His voice becomes unmistakable to us.

WORK IT OUT

To smile without fear of the future, I need to exchange the *fear of the future* for the *fear of the LORD*.

Read through the "Spend Time with Your Father" assessment at the end of this week. After completing it, consider what is most attainable for you:

Is there a time of day that makes more sense for you—morning, lunchtime, evening, or small pockets of time throughout the day?

Is there a place that is easy for you to get to—your closet, your bedroom, your desk at work, or even your car?

After you answer these questions, write down how you would like to begin weaving this pattern of spending time with your Father into your everyday life. Then give it a trial run. Don't be disappointed if it doesn't work out just as you planned. Allow God to shape it as you show up each day.

_____

_____

_____

_____

_____

_____

_____

_____

_____

_____

_____

_____

_____

_____

_____

_____

I Have a Plan

Memory Verse

You did not ___*receive*___ the spirit of ___*fear*___ to fall back into ___*slavery*___, but you have ___*received*___ the Spirit of ___*adoption*___ ___*as sons of God*___ by whom we cry, "Abba! Father!"

Romans 8:15

"Katy, why is there a can of hair spray and a T-ball bat next to your bed?"

After a few weeks away, my husband came home and uncovered my emergency plan. Home alone with six small children in a large, unfamiliar city, I thought it important to have a plan. Sure, I could pick up the phone and call for help, but I needed something for the gap between when I called and when it showed up. Enter the T-ball bat and hair spray. Should an intruder enter the house, I figured I'd blind him with the hair spray, then smack him with the bat. It was foolproof. At least I thought so. Apparently, Luke didn't agree.

Your ability to recognize God's voice will have a direct impact on your willingness to trust His choices. When we know God personally and progressively, as we talked about yesterday, we can trust Him no matter what we face. And that's important because the future is full of uncertainties. They're not going anywhere. If anything, they're growing more numerous and more threatening by the day.

What is certain is that we will, at some point in our lives, find ourselves in the middle of a situation we never hoped or prayed for. We'll face circumstances that we may have done everything in our power to avoid. In order to exchange the fear of the future for the fear of the LORD, we need a plan today for how we will handle tomorrow. And I don't mean a T-ball bat and hair spray.

Remember the story of my son Jonah on the ropes course? I want you to consider your life as though you were in Jonah's place. If you were frozen in fear on the course of life, whose voice would you most likely identify with God's voice? Using the metaphor of Jonah's dilemma, you have four options:

1. The brother's or sister's voice
2. The instructor's voice
3. The onlooker's voice
4. The father's voice

Only one of these four voices was able to help my son in his moment of fear. Let's look at them a little closer to find out why.

Consider the brother's or sister's voice. Is God's voice like this to you? A familiar voice, for sure—one you might even enjoy hearing—but not one you always follow, because you haven't given it a position of authority in your life.

Is God's voice like that of the instructor? You believe He has answers because He's an expert on this course you walk, but you struggle to trust Him because you don't really know Him.

What about the onlooker? In Jonah's case, this was my voice. Maybe you can faintly hear God's voice and even draw a little comfort from it, but it's so far removed from your life that His instructions and encouragement never make it to the ears of your heart.

The best option—the one that will lead you to trust God's choices—is when God's voice is as close as Luke's voice was to Jonah that day. A voice that is near you. The voice of the One who sees you. A voice that you know will guide you in love. A voice that you know will never leave you.

Which voice best describes God's voice in your life right now? Why?

onlooker ~ Father

The woman in Proverbs 31 smiles without fear of the future—not because of earthly security or stability but because of whom she trusts. To exchange fear of the future for fear of the LORD, we have to not only know God's voice but also trust His choices.

When we can't see how God's will is being worked out in our lives, we can still trust that His plan is good.

DIGGING IN

I'm not sure how I know this, but I've heard that if you ever find yourself in quicksand, you shouldn't struggle to get out. Instead, experts say to lean back very slowly so that you are almost floating on your back.

How unnatural that must be! It only makes sense that if you feel the sand pulling you under, you should try to break free at any cost. To struggle to get out! But while it may seem scary, experts say that if you lean into it, you will float. It's when you try to stand in the quicksand and struggle against it that you sink.

We're not likely to encounter literal quicksand, but the circumstances we face can certainly feel like it. When we find ourselves in these circumstantial pits, it's natural to strive for a way out. But when the quicksand of life closes in around us, we have to surrender instead of struggle.

David wrote, "Into your hand I commit my spirit; you have redeemed me, O LORD, faithful God" (Ps. 31:5).

The events of David's life are well chronicled in Scripture, and when we meet David in Psalm 31, he seems to be in the quicksand of life. He was no stranger to struggle. From his time as a shepherd boy to the time of his death, David faced circumstances that threatened to swallow him. Psalm 31 details his response to one of these sandpits.

Some scholars point to Keilah as the besieged city mentioned in verse 21. David and his band of men had conquered a Philistine army and saved the people of Keilah. But Israel's King Saul, feeling threatened by David, sent an expedition to attack the city. David and his men fled from Keilah into the wilderness and stayed there (see 1 Sam. 23). And "Saul sought him every day, but God did not give him into his hand" (v. 14).

Whether the siege of Keilah or other events had set the stage for this psalm, David must have wondered where his life had taken a wrong turn. After all, Samuel had anointed David as the next king of Israel. Then, one chapter after his anointing, David caught the attention of King Saul when he took down the Philistine champion, Goliath (see 1 Sam. 16–17). But now, instead of the plush palace, David found himself hiding in wilderness strongholds on the run from a mad king.

Psalm 31 gives us a glimpse into the depths of David's despair:

> I will rejoice and be glad in your steadfast love,
>   because you have seen my affliction;
>   you have known the distress of my soul,
> and you have not delivered me into the hand of the enemy;
>   you have set my feet in a broad place.
>
>
> Be gracious to me, O LORD, for I am in distress;
>   my eye is wasted from grief;
>   my soul and my body also.
> For my life is spent with sorrow,
>   and my years with sighing;
> my strength fails because of my iniquity,
>   and my bones waste away. (vv. 7–10)

His soul was distressed (v. 7). His eye, soul, and body were wasted from grief (v. 9). His life was spent in sorrow, his years were spent with sighing, and his strength was failing (v. 10). That's an all-around bad day.

Describe a time when you've felt like David.

David, God's anointed, felt forgotten and useless. Yet in the midst of despair, he surrendered to God. Instead of fixing his eyes on all that seemed wrong around him, David continued to hope in God's goodness and steadfast love.

We can find in David's cry a pattern to apply to our own situational quicksand. Let's look at three steps for trusting God in any circumstances:

1. Start with God.

> You are my rock and my fortress;
>   and for your name's sake you lead me and guide me;
> you take me out of the net they have hidden for me,
>   for you are my refuge. (vv. 3–4)

Circle the three things David said God is for him. (Hint: they all follow the word *my*.) Underline the three things David expected God to do for him.

When we start with God, His truth shifts our perspective from what we fear to His limitless provision.

2. Filter fear through truth.

> I will rejoice and be glad in your steadfast love,
>   because you have seen my affliction;
>   you have known the distress of my soul,
> and you have not delivered me into the hand of the enemy;
>   you have set my feet in a broad place. (vv. 7–8)

In the midst of uncertain circumstances, David made a decision to dwell on God's stead-fast love. In doing so, he rejoiced in knowing that God saw him, God knew him, and God protected him. When we filter our fears through God's Word and character, we too can rely on His faithfulness and rest in His love.

3. Give your burden about the outcome to God.

> I trust in you, O LORD;
>   I say, "You are my God."
> My times are in your hand;
>   rescue me from the hand of my enemies and from my persecutors!
>   (vv. 14–15)

By all accounts, David didn't look for a T-ball bat or a can of hair spray to handle his adversaries. Instead, he relied fully on God—on His plan and His ability to rescue him. As God's child, any attack on you is a direct attack on your heavenly Father and His Son, Jesus. And with that, we can take heart, because He has overcome the world (see John 16:33)!

As His final words before He gave up His life on the cross, our Savior, Jesus, prayed Psalm 31:5:

> Jesus, calling out with a loud voice, said, "Father, into your hands I commit
> my spirit!" And having said this he breathed his last. (Luke 23:46)

Jesus endured this path for the joy of accomplishing His Father's will. And though it wasn't always clear to human eyes, God's path culminated in Jesus seated in victory at the right hand of God's throne.

When we can't see how God's will is being worked out in our lives, we can still trust that His plan is good. When our circumstances take us places we wouldn't have chosen, we too can choose to hope in God's goodness and love.

Yes, in the midst of our own desperate circumstances, releasing our lives completely to God can feel scary. That's why it's so important to know His voice. In these circumstantial pits of life, we must trust His choices enough to lean back into our faithful God, confident that He will keep us afloat. It's when we try to stand on our own that we risk sinking.

WORK IT OUT

> ✂ **To smile without fear of the future, I need to exchange the** *fear of the future* **for the** *fear of the LORD.* ✂

Go back to week 1, day 1 of our study, and review your list of fears of the future. Pick one (or all) of those circumstances, and apply the pattern of trusting God to them. Write out a prayer that starts with truth about who God is; then filter each fear through that truth. You may want to reference some of the verses from the "Keep Your Heart" tool at the end of week 1.

Once you've done that, bow your head and bend your knee, allowing your burden about the results of this situation to roll off your shoulders and fall at the feet of Jesus.

Day 5

A Woman Who Fears the Lord

Memory Verse

You did not _receive_ the spirit of _fear_ to fall back into _slavery_, but you have _received_ the Spirit of _adoption_ _as sons_, by whom we cry, "_Abba_! _Father_!"

Romans 8:15

Turn to the book of Exodus, and read chapter 1.

Exodus opens with Israel, God's chosen people, living as slaves in Egypt. The final fourteen chapters of the book of Genesis detail how they got there.

Exodus 1:15 names two women who feared God. What are their names? In what role did they serve?

Based on what we learn in Exodus 1, what kind of ruler do you think the new pharaoh was? (vv. 10–11, 16)

How did the midwives exchange the fear of the future for the fear of the LORD?

According to Exodus 1:20–21, what happened to the midwives because they feared God?

What happened to the nation of Israel?

Because of the hostility of the culture in which they found themselves, it would have been safer for the midwives if they had followed Pharaoh's orders. But they knew the Egyptian king's orders were in direct opposition to what pleased God. Therefore, they had a choice to make.

The decision to follow God was highly dangerous, but because the midwives feared God and not humans, God rewarded them with families. In the ancient world, a family brought great security and hope for the future. Without one, women were vulnerable and most likely poor.

I love how the Voice translation renders Exodus 1:20: "God was good to the midwives, and *under their care* the Israelite women had many more children. *Despite Pharaoh's orders,* the people of Israel became stronger and more powerful."[1]

The midwives' choice to obey God affected their own lives, but it also impacted the entire nation of Israel. Despite Pharaoh's attempts to destroy God's people, God sustained them and even increased their strength and power. And the two women who feared the LORD were the conduit for His blessing and provision.

WORK IT OUT

> ✂ To smile without fear of the future, I need to exchange the *fear of the future* for the *fear of the* LORD. ✂

Use the space below to work through what you've learned this week. How have you been challenged or convicted? What do you want to do differently after this week of study? Is there anything unsettled in your heart?

_____

_____

_____

_____

_____

_____

_____

_____

_____

_____

_____

_____

_____

_____

_____

We've done a lot of work this week. I pray that you are encouraged and excited to begin exchanging the fear of the future for the fear of the LORD.

Spend Time with Your Father

Use this tool to help determine how and when you can spend time with God and grow progressively and personally in your knowledge of Him.

Evaluate Your Discretionary Time

Consider these questions:

- How much time do you spend reading books, magazines, or online articles?
- How much time do you spend scrolling on social media?
- How much time do you spend making nonwork phone calls or texting with friends?
- How much time do you spend watching television or YouTube?
- How much time do you spend engaging in hobbies?

Evaluate Your Life Stage

Consider these questions:

- Do you have small children at home and therefore no two days are the same?
- Do you have aging parents or a sick family member whose needs often require your immediate time and attention?
- Do you have a job that requires you to pack up and move to new locations often or suddenly?
- Do you have a job or home life that presents a consistent, structured pattern?

Evaluate Your Learning Style

Consider these questions:

- When are you most alert? First thing in the morning? Midmorning? In the evening when everyone else is winding down?
- When are you most engaged? When listening to a speaker or during conversation with others? When watching a video? When reading a book?

See the next page for suggestions and ideas based on your answers.

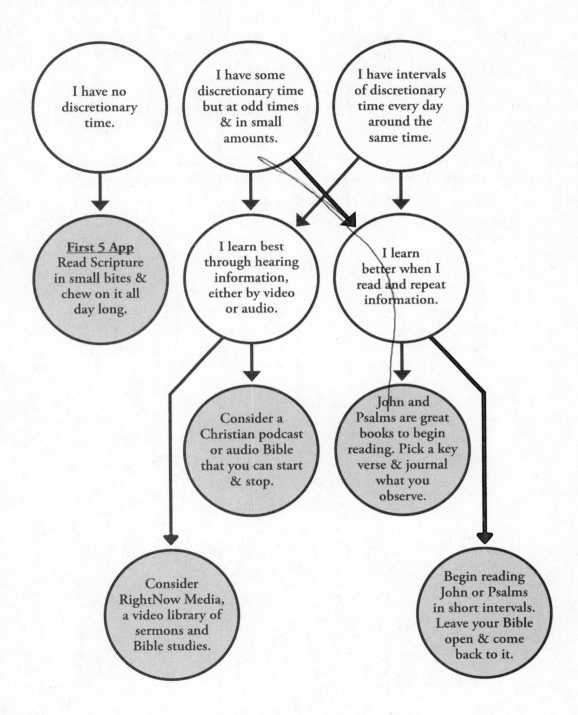

Video Session 3:
Her Heart's Position

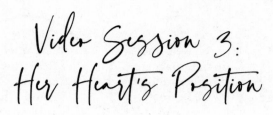

Watch video session 3, and use this space to write notes or record insights.

Week 3

Her Heart's Preparation: Living Confident

leaf illustration

Memory Verse

Be strong in the Lord and in the strength of his might.

Ephesians 6:10

Introduction

That's impossible.

As he rounded the corner, he was all alone.

He didn't look back. He didn't worry about how far he had to go. With his eyes fixed on the finish line, he ran. Faster and faster and faster.

The movie *Secretariat* has become one of my all-time favorites. It details the events surrounding a horse named Secretariat and his quest to win the Triple Crown, a series of three races in less than two months' time. Many believed it couldn't be done. Secretariat, they said, was a speed horse, built to run fast but not far.

The year was 1973, and the race was the Belmont Stakes, the final race of the Triple Crown. Often called the "Test of the Champion,"[1] it is the longest of the three tracks.

On the day of the final race, only four other horses dared to challenge Secretariat, as most conceded it to be a two-horse race between Secretariat and his rival, Sham.

Sham's team had a plan to defeat Secretariat—push him to run too fast at the beginning of the race so he would wear out early, slow down, and ultimately lose the race. And that's exactly what they tried.

At the sound of the bell, the gates opened and Sham and Secretariat burst onto the track. Secretariat wore his trademark blue-and-white-checkered mask, matching the jersey of his jockey perched atop his strong back. Secretariat surged forward to join the leaders, a move uncharacteristic for him. In earlier races, he had hung back, then made a final push to the finish line, leaving the rest of the racers in his dust. But not today.

Sham and Secretariat raced side by side as they rounded the first turn of the track, while the other three horses tried in vain to keep up. Onlookers believed the fast start to be a catastrophe for Secretariat, while Sham's team smiled with delight. Their plan appeared to be unfolding exactly as they had hoped.

Except Secretariat never slowed down.

Sham pushed him faster, and he ran faster. Sham ran even faster, yet Secretariat still kept up.

As the horses entered the final half mile of the race, it was Sham who slowed down, while Secretariat continued to accelerate.

Secretariat won the race that day by a record-breaking thirty-one lengths. He became the first Triple Crown winner in twenty-five years, and his world records for time and margin of victory still stand today. As he rounded the final turn of the track, he ran all alone at a blazing speed that no one thought was possible.

In the movie, as Sham's trainer watches Secretariat pull away, he utters two words: "That's impossible."[2]

Day 1

Unlimited Strength

Memory Verse
Be strong in the Lord and in the strength of his might.
Ephesians 6:10

I'm going to be honest with you. Of all the parts of this study, this week has been one of the hardest to write. You'll find out more about why as we go along each day, but to sum up, I like to be strong. When I don't feel strong, I at least like to look like I am strong. Maybe you understand.

There seems to be a trend in our culture today that elevates strength to a new high. These messages tell us that all we need for life is on the inside and all we have to do is tap into it. We read slogans like "You've got it in you" and "Strong is the new pretty." At first glance, they seem okay—even good. I saw a T-shirt that read, "I can do all things." You may have detected something missing from that statement, but I think the makers of the shirt left it off intentionally. (Hint: check out Philippians 4:13.)

What we study this week kind of messes up this message, because ultimately what we will learn is that we, in and of ourselves, actually can't do all things.

We *have* been given a strength and dignity that can never be taken from us. It's not the kind that wears out or comes and goes. It's the kind that does things in us and through us that cause us (and the people around us) to say things like "That's impossible." But walking in this strength and dignity will require something from us.

I don't know what time of day you're reading this. I don't know what day of the week it is or what the weather is like, but I'm going to make an assumption: no matter where you are or what time it is, I am going to assume that you are wearing clothes … at least some form of them.

What did you put on when you woke up this morning? This isn't a trick question.

Since that dreadful moment in Genesis 3, the practice of humanity has been to clothe ourselves to cover our nakedness. Consequently, the norm of society is to wake up, get out of bed, and put something on our bodies. What we clothe ourselves with, however, varies.

In the space above, you may have written a number of different things. If you're a nurse, you may have written that you put on scrubs this morning. If you're a teacher, maybe you wrote "comfortable shoes." If you're a stay-at-home mom, you may have put on the shirt you wore yesterday because it's just going to get stained again today and that's one less bit of laundry to wash, fold, and put away.

If you work at the post office or in the military, maybe you described your uniform. If you are headed to the gym, you likely put on fitness clothes. Or if you aren't going anywhere at all, you may still be clothed in your pajamas—you can write that down too.

My guess is that whatever you put on this morning was determined by your planned activity for the day.

The Proverbs 31 woman also gets dressed for the day: "Strength and dignity are her clothing, and she smiles at the future" (v. 25 NASB). She is clothed with strength and dignity.

Strength and dignity are not physical pieces of clothing that can be purchased at a department store or online with free two-day shipping. However, the Hebrew word translated "clothing" in this verse is the same word used to describe a physical garment—something you put on your body. It implies something you wrap around yourself.

I love the way the Amplified Bible translates this verse:

Strength and dignity are her clothing *and* her position is strong and secure; she rejoices over the future [the latter day or time to come, knowing that she and her family are in readiness for it]! (AMPC)

Can you see the progression described here?

Because strength and dignity are her clothing ———➤ her position is strong and secure.

Because her position is strong and secure ———➤ she knows she is ready for the future.

Because she knows she is ready for the future ———➤ she rejoices over it.

The woman in Proverbs 31 can smile without fear of the future because she's ready for it. Not ready in the sense that she has considered every possible what-if scenario and made a plan to handle it. No, this kind of preparation starts on the inside.

She has dressed her heart in such a way that she has full confidence that she is prepared for the future. When we think about living prepared for the future, we often consider all the outward defenses and arrangements necessary to live in security and confidence. But for the Proverbs 31 woman, it is the preparation of her heart that produces confidence for the future.

In your attempts to prepare for the future, how have you prepared your heart?

Do you believe that you could prepare your heart for anything? Why or why not?

DIGGING IN

The Hebrew words translated "strength" and "dignity" in Proverbs 31:25 are `oz and *hadar*. They are paired together in only two other places in the Old Testament. Let's look at those two other verses:

> Splendor and majesty are before him;
>   strength and joy are in his place. (1 Chron. 16:27)

> Splendor and majesty are before him;
>   strength and beauty are in his sanctuary. (Ps. 96:6)

Both of these verses are a part of songs of thanksgiving and worship to the Lord. In both verses, just as in Proverbs 31:25, `oz is translated "strength."[1] However, whereas the Hebrew word *hadar* is translated "dignity" in Proverbs 31:25, both verses translate *hadar* as "majesty."[2]

Where do both of these verses say you can find *hadar* (dignity)?

Where do they say `oz (strength) is found?

The strength and dignity that clothe the woman in Proverbs 31:25 are not a result of her long list of works. She didn't earn this strength and dignity, and she didn't produce them. Instead, strength and dignity have been *placed on her* as she dwells in the presence of God.

Read Proverbs 18:10: "The name of the LORD is a strong tower; the righteous man runs into it and is safe."

The Bible gives us several different names for the Lord. As we begin this process of relying on Him for our strength, I think knowing at least some of those names will help us. I've included a short list below of some of the names of God given to us in the Old Testament.[3] Each name is followed by a definition and a reference where it is mentioned.

NAME OF GOD	WHAT IT MEANS	WHERE IT'S FOUND IN SCRIPTURE
Yahweh Elyon	The LORD Most High	Psalm 91:1
Yahweh Yir'eh	The LORD will provide	Genesis 22:14
Yahweh Nissi	The LORD is my banner	Exodus 17:15
Yahweh Rohi	The LORD is my shepherd	Psalm 23:1
Yahweh Rophe	The LORD, your healer	Exodus 15:26
Yahweh Shalom	The LORD is peace	Judges 6:24
Yahweh Shammah	The LORD is there	Ezekiel 48:35

Wow, there are hardly words for what we've just read. I know this list comes toward the end of the day's study, and I know it's simply a list with only a reference for each name. But this could be the most powerful point of the entire study.

I encourage you not to rush through this list. Slow down. Digest it. Look up the verses, and let each name of God sink into your heart.

Which name or names of the Lord minister most to you in your current circumstances?

How does knowing these names of the Lord change how you view the future?

Last week, we learned to cry out with the words, "God, I'm scared!" This week, we need to learn to turn to God for our strength, and that starts with a declaration of submission: "God, I can't!"

Consider what we stand to gain when we trade our own attempts to be strong for the strength of the Lord. Our strength is limited; the strength of the Lord is unlimited. Our strength reaches only as far as we can see; God's strength sees what we can't see and prepares us for what we don't know is coming. Our strength increases and decreases based on what we face and our physical condition at the moment; God is all powerful and remains the same yesterday, today, and forever.

As we close today, let's settle this. Every day we can open our eyes and be sure of one thing: no matter what today holds, no matter what the future holds, we need Jesus. As we learned in week 1, apart from Him we can do nothing (see John 15:5). But as we will see this week, with Him all things are possible.

WORK IT OUT

As you consider the names of the Lord, think about the differences between the strength we try to produce on our own and the strength of the Lord. Use the table below to record some of the contrasts you come up with.

MY STRENGTH	THE STRENGTH OF THE LORD

Day 2

The Secret to Strength

Memory Verse

Be strong _in   the   Lord_ and in the strength of his might.
Ephesians 6:10

I didn't know whether to cry or laugh. The nurse's words rang in my ears: "The doctor wants you in the bed." My doctor ordered me to park myself in my bed for the sake of my unborn child.

Moments earlier, I had packed up my four children, all under the age of six, in a bit of a rush. I knew something wasn't right, and when I called my doctor, she advised me to come to her office immediately. An ultrasound revealed the problem. A hemorrhage—almost seven times larger than a normal hemorrhage would be—threatened to harm both our baby and me.

As I gazed at the four smiling little faces nearby, the reality of the situation swirled through my thoughts like leaves on a windy day. We lived thousands of miles from family. Luke's work schedule was rigid and exhausting. And we didn't have many close friends to speak of. I'm pretty sure my mouth was open, yet no words would form, and I definitely don't remember blinking. Then, in an out-of-body type moment, I looked at the nurse and declared, "God will provide." I'm not positive I believed it.

I fastened some children into the double stroller, and we slowly made the long walk back to the parking garage. I loaded my little ones into the car, and we drove home. When we pulled into the driveway, I settled my energetic bunch before I crawled into bed and the floodgates of my emotions opened wide.

Question after question crossed my mind, and I argued with God: *How can this possibly honor You more, God? How can I possibly serve You better from this bed than on my feet? Who will take care of my family, God?*

Have you ever had a good day? You know, those days when you're just on. Those days when no matter what comes your way, you feel like you can handle it. Those "I got this" kind of days.

Describe yourself on your best day. What does your hair look like? How are you dressed? What does your house look like? Your car? Your desk at work? What do you eat for dinner?

Admittedly, I like talking about my best days. But in order to make the point I'm going to make, we have to consider another question: Have you ever had a bad day? You know, the days when nothing seems to go right. The "I wish I'd stayed in bed" kind of days.

Describe yourself on your worst day—the opposite day of the one you just described.

Based on these two descriptions, on which day would you say you are clothed with strength and dignity?

I'm going to guess you picked your best day. Who wouldn't feel strong when everything seems to be going right? When we can point to people, places, and things that seem to prove we have everything together, we often feel like we are handling life well. And when we handle life well, we feel strong. Therefore, those days, our best days, must be the days when we operate in strength and dignity. On our worst days, on the other hand, we feel defeated, accused, and like all-out failures.

But what if I told you that not only could be you operating in strength and dignity on what you call your *worst* day, but you could actually *not* be operating in strength and dignity on your best day?

> Charm is deceitful, and beauty is vain,
>> but a woman who fears the LORD is to be praised. (Prov. 31:30)

We studied the last part of this verse in-depth last week. Today I want to look at the first part. Circle what this verse calls deceitful, and underline what it says is vain.

We usually identify someone as charming based on how she acts. It could be her smile or charisma or overall presence that captures a crowd.

After mentioning charm, this verse makes a statement about beauty. We identify someone as beautiful based on how she looks. Often beauty is subjective and can change with the winds of the culture. Nevertheless, beauty typically refers to appearance.

Based on this understanding of charm and beauty, we could read the verse like this: "Actions are deceitful, and appearances are vain, but a woman who fears the LORD is to be praised."

Now read Proverbs 31:25 again: "Strength and dignity are her clothing, and she smiles at the future" (NASB).

If actions are deceiving and appearances are vain, we must assume that the strength and dignity the Proverbs 31 woman clothes herself in are not woven with the threads of what she does or how she looks. And if that is the case, then our assessment of when we live clothed in strength and dignity cannot be tied to our best days or our worst days.

If we are going to live clothed in strength and dignity, then we're going to have to change our definition of strength and dignity.

DIGGING IN

Read 2 Corinthians 12:9–10:

> [The Lord] said to me, "My grace is sufficient for you, for my power is made perfect in weakness." Therefore I will boast all the more gladly of my weaknesses, so that the power of Christ may rest upon me. For the sake of Christ, then, I am content with weaknesses, insults, hardships, persecutions, and calamities. For when I am weak, then I am strong.

The Greek word translated "boast" in this verse means "to glory in a thing."[1] The word translated "weakness" is *astheneia* and means "feebleness of mind or body."[2]

For a long time I applied this verse to my life the wrong way. I talked about my deficiencies, saying things like "I am a terrible artist. I can't even draw stick figures!" Or "I am technologically challenged. I just learned how to send emails to more than one person at the same time." I believed that statements like these were examples of obeying this Scripture and "boasting" in my weaknesses.

But here's the thing. I wasn't trying to draw stick figures. My daily life didn't require me to do art. And when I needed something techy done, I called someone else to do it. These so-called weaknesses didn't require me to look for and lean on God's strength. They weren't really weaknesses at all.

Are there certain weaknesses in your life that you don't mind boasting about? List a few.

It wasn't until I became weak in areas where I thought I should be strong that I began to understand what it meant for Jesus' power to be made perfect in my weakness.

During those weeks I spent on bed rest, my circumstances forced me to surrender the places in which I'd believed myself to be strong. Before bed rest, I had found pride in what I could provide my family as a wife and mother. I had assessed my success based on things like a clean house, well-behaved children, and a happy husband. On my best days, when I had cooked dinner, folded laundry, and loaded the dishwasher, I lay down at night pleased with myself and my ability.

Oh, but did you catch that? I felt good about myself and my ability. On what I called my best days, I was actually operating in my own strength, not God's. The result of those days was praise and elevation of myself, not God.

To smile without fear of the future, I need to rely on my Savior instead of myself.

When God positioned me so I could not do any of the things by which I had labeled myself strong, it forced me to rely on His strength. It was from there, flat on my back, that I realized we can claim to live in the power of Christ while deep down relying on our own strength.

To help us identify the heart infection of self-reliance, let's look at a few of its symptoms:

- Your thoughts swarm around your to-do list all day.
- You say things like "I'm fine" or "I've got this."
- You'd rather walk across hot coals than ask someone for help.
- When life gets hectic, the time you spend with your Father is the first thing you drop.

Are you experiencing any of these symptoms?

Which ones are most common in your life?

The last symptom on that list convicts me. Somehow when I feel like I need to be strong, my instincts push me to do more. The checklist is long, and expectations are high, so to spend less time doing and more time being with Jesus feels unproductive.

But if we truly rely on the power of Christ, the time we spend with Him will be our lifeline. When our schedules fill up or situations pile up, instead of quickly dismissing the time we spend in God's Word and prayer, we will search for any minutes to shut the door and take refuge in the Word. Which brings us to step three:

> ✂ **To smile without fear of the future, I need to rely on my Savior instead of myself.** ✂

During my bed rest days, something special happened. As I surrendered, God supplied His strength.

I still hosted a weekly women's Bible study. Every Thursday, I moved from the bed to the couch and joined a group of women around God's Word. I never knew how clean my house would or wouldn't be. I wasn't the perfect hostess. There were never snacks laid out or fresh flowers on the table or hot coffee. Most days, I met them in my sweatpants and without makeup. But it didn't matter. Why? Because Katy McCown wasn't the one on display. Jesus Christ was.

As God's power was made perfect in my weakness, the women at the Bible study didn't see *me* and they didn't praise my works. They saw God's power at work within me. And they praised Him. In surrender and humility, I could finally live clothed in the strength and dignity of Jesus.

Our surrender swings open the door to God's strength.

That is the true definition of this strength and dignity we're studying. If you are in Christ, you have admitted that you are a sinner in need of a Savior and have believed in your heart and confessed with your mouth that Jesus is Lord (see Rom. 10:9). Therefore, you already possess this strength and dignity. If you are not yet in Christ, this strength and dignity have already been purchased for you. You simply have to receive them through faith in Christ.

WORK IT OUT

> ✄ **To smile without fear of the future, I need to rely on my Savior instead of myself.** ✄

The sickness of self-reliance can show itself in two ways: by all the things we take on our own shoulders and rely on ourselves to solve, fix, or arrange, and by all the things we refuse to take on because we can't figure out how to solve, fix, or arrange them.

In either situation, we are allowing an inaccurate definition of strength to control the present and dictate the future. As we close today, spend some time with God, and ask Him to begin revealing to you the people, decisions, and rhythms of your life that are being impacted by self-reliance.

Use the space below to record a prayer of repentance and express your desire to rely fully on God's power at work within you.

_____

_____

_____

_____

_____

_____

_____

_____

_____

Our surrender swings open the door to God's strength.

The Relief of Relying on God

Memory Verse

Be strong _____ _____ _____

and in the _____ *of his might.*

Ephesians 6:10

It's possible I had never searched the internet more in my entire life.

After a serious and unpredictable medical diagnosis of a loved one, I made it my mission to figure out the future. I felt sure that with the right combination of symptoms and information, I would land on the answer to what was causing the problems. And if I knew what caused the condition, then I could share with the medical professionals how to fix it.

In every spare minute, I turned to my phone or computer. But no matter how hard I tried, I could not land on a concrete answer. My search proved more frustrating than freeing, and I finished more confused than comforted.

When we read verse after verse about the productivity of the Proverbs 31 woman, it can feel like a few verses are missing. Because when a woman carries that much of a load, she tends to get a little edgy. So where, might I ask, is the verse that says, "She often feels frustrated and frantic, but she hides it well"? Or the one that says, "Every now and then, her smile fades to a scowl, and you'd better just do what she says, but it's usually only when she's running late"?

Attempting all that she does in her own strength would surely produce sentiments like those I just described. But they aren't there. I've checked … multiple times. Now, that's not to say she's not strong. As a matter of fact, the Proverbs 31 woman "dresses herself with strength and makes her arms strong" (v. 17).

The word for "strength" in this verse is the same word we've studied that is used in verse 25. However, in this context "it probably means that she is physically capable of doing hard work."[1]

In fact, there is a noteworthy emphasis on strength in the twenty-two verses that describe the Proverbs 31 woman. So much so that some scholars believe Proverbs 31:10–31 to be part of Israel's heroic poetry—ancient writings that recount a hero's deeds and are usually connected to military exploits.[2]

The issue here is not whether she is physically strong or able. Instead, the issue is what she chooses to rely on. To do what she does the way she does it, she cannot possibly rely on her own ability. As we discussed earlier this week, her strength is limited.

DIGGING IN

To learn more about relying on our Savior instead of ourselves, let's visit the scene of an Old Testament battlefield.

Read 2 Chronicles 13. Who are the two main characters?

Abijah and Jeroboam

This chapter introduces us to King Abijah. Aside from eight verses in 1 Kings 15 and two verses in 2 Chronicles 11, this chapter gives us the only biblical information about this king and his life. One event. One battle. One speech. But, boy, is it a good one.

The Hebrew word translated "relied" in verse 18 is *sha'an*. It means "to lean on." This word is used in other places in the Old Testament to communicate the idea of leaning on a spear or a person for support. However, in this verse, *sha'an* communicates a much stronger idea. *A Dictionary of Biblical Languages* defines it as "[to] have trust and belief in an object to the point of being in jeopardy if the object of trust fails."[3]

I once watched a live television broadcast of a man who dared to cross a gorge near the Grand Canyon on a tightrope … without a net. This had disaster written all over it. Of course, the man had prepared for this event. He was a professional tightrope walker. Still, it seemed like he would have had some kind of a backup plan. Something that, should the unexpected happen, would save him from sure death. But he didn't.

I could hardly watch. I hid behind my living room wall and peeked out just enough to make sure the man hadn't fallen. The wind blew, sometimes so hard he actually had to squat on the rope and wait for the gusts to calm. Even recounting his walk makes my stomach uneasy. It was dangerous and came with real, irreversible consequences should it go wrong.

But it didn't go wrong. Despite my doubts, the man made it safely across and ran into the embrace of his family waiting on the other side.[4]

In today's chapter Abijah appears to have been crossing his own tightrope of trust. Outmanned two to one, Abijah and his army stood their ground because of one belief: "God is with us at our head" (2 Chron. 13:12). And because they relied on the Lord, "the men of Judah prevailed" (v. 18).

One scholar described this kind of reliance as "trust and conscious dependence on God."[5] If we want to consciously depend on God, it will be helpful to know the things we tend to rely on instead of Him.

When we rely on God, we receive relief from the burden of figuring out the future.

Look up the verses below, and write down what God instructed His people *not* to lean on:

Isaiah 31:1 ⟶ ~~horses~~ men

Job 8:15 ⟶ home

Proverbs 3:5 ⟶ thine own understanding

Circle which of these you are most likely to rely on instead of God.

Job 8:15 and Isaiah 31:1 describe people and physical resources as things that will not stand if we choose to rely on them. Proverbs 3:5 lists another false foundation to avoid: "Do not lean on your own understanding." Another way to say this could be "Don't try to figure everything out on your own."[6]

Of all the things listed above, I think this is the one I struggle with most. When my loved one got sick, I relied on my own understanding. I knew that God was in control, and I believed He had the power to heal and help. But I wanted to know for myself. Researching it all myself gave me a sense of control over the situation. In 2 Chronicles 13 we see these two opposite positions: reliance on God and reliance on self.

Read 2 Chronicles 13:18. Who did Abijah, king of Judah, rely on?

Now read verses 8 and 13. Who or what did Jeroboam, king of Israel, rely on?

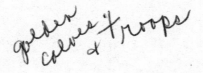

Jeroboam had a good plan. He set up an ambush to attack Judah from behind and had soldiers ready to attack in front (see v. 13). He had more mighty warriors than Abijah had (see v. 3). And he had set up for himself a system for worshipping false gods (see vv. 8–9). Based on his own understanding, Jeroboam had Judah surrounded, signaling sure success.

Abijah, however, relied on God. Abijah followed the law set forth by God in allowing only sons of Aaron to serve as priests and only Levites to serve at the temple (see Ex. 30:30; Num. 3:5–9). He followed God's instructions for burnt offerings, the showbread, and the lampstand (see Ex. 25:30; 29:38–39; Lev. 24:2–3). And when Abijah took his army into battle, he acknowledged the ways of God by having his priests blow their battle trumpets first (see Num. 10:8–9). Because he obeyed God, he could confidently say, "O sons of Israel, do not fight against the LORD, the God of your fathers, for you cannot succeed" (2 Chron. 13:12).

When we seek to figure things out on our own, the burden of the results rests on our shoulders. We are forced to rely on our own limited resources. When we rely on God, we receive relief from the burden of figuring out the future. As we acknowledge God in all our ways, He is faithful to direct our steps (see Prov. 3:6).

When we rely on our Savior instead of ourselves, we experience true strength and dignity.

The writer of Chronicles was intentional in his emphasis on war and the process of victory or defeat. He knew his audience would face military threats as they returned to their homeland, and he wanted to make sure they remembered that God was their only way to victory. He taught his readers how to avoid defeat and secure the blessing of victory in battle.[7]

Much like the original readers of 2 Chronicles, we too are cautioned about a struggle not only against flesh and blood but also against the rulers and principalities in the heavenly realms. But we need not fear the battle, because God gives us everything we need to be strong in Him and stand against our enemies. (In the passage below, I've left the verse numbers in to help you answer the questions that follow.)

> [10]Be strong in the Lord and in the strength of his might. [11]Put on the whole armor of God, that you may be able to stand against the schemes of the devil. [12]For we do not wrestle against flesh and blood, but against the rulers, against the authorities, against the cosmic powers over this present darkness, against the spiritual forces of evil in the heavenly places. [13]Therefore take up the whole armor of God, that you may be able to withstand in the evil day, and having done all, to stand firm. [14]Stand therefore, having fastened

on the belt of truth, and having put on the breastplate of righteousness, [15]and, as shoes for your feet, having put on the readiness given by the gospel of peace. [16]In all circumstances take up the shield of faith, with which you can extinguish all the flaming darts of the evil one; [17]and take the helmet of salvation, and the sword of the Spirit, which is the word of God, [18]praying at all times in the Spirit, with all prayer and supplication. (Eph. 6:10–18)

What does verse 11 say we are to put on?

Why does it say we should put this on?

Ephesians 6:14–17 details six pieces of armor God gives us to put on daily:

- **The belt of truth** to secure us and alert us to be on guard so that we are not tripped up by lies.
- **The breastplate of righteousness** to guard our hearts, which are the wellspring of life, and to remind us that we cannot create our own righteousness through good works.
- **The gospel of peace as shoes** to keep our steps steady, no matter what kind of path we travel.
- **The shield of faith** to protect us and link us together as a unified body in Christ.
- **The helmet of salvation** to guard our minds and transform our thoughts.
- **The sword of the Spirit**, God's Word, so that we may advance. This is our preferred weapon when the enemy wants us to fight like the world,

repaying evil for evil, taking matters into our own hands, and lashing out, instead of persisting in love and grace.

During those days with my sick loved one, as I wrestled with the desire to figure everything out, God comforted me with the truth that His grace is sufficient for me (see 2 Cor. 12:9). I set my heart and mind on worshipping God instead of wandering through countless websites. And as I relied on God, I found the strength to continue.

When we remain in Christ, we learn to revere Him. As we revere Him, we learn to rely on Him. And as we rely on our Savior instead of on ourselves, we experience true strength and dignity.

WORK IT OUT

> ✼ **To smile without fear of the future, I need to rely on my Savior instead of myself.** ✼

At the end of this week's study, you will find a resource titled "Thirteen Hangers for Your Heart." Read through the spiritual garments that God provides for us to clothe ourselves with.

After you've done that, come back here and, thinking of your heart as a closet, consider these questions: *Are any of these spiritual clothes not in my heart's closet? Have any of these spiritual garments been pushed to the back of my heart's closet? Maybe I have them but I'm not putting them on each day. Are there any spiritual clothes that I need to learn more about in order to wear them properly?*

Day 4

When You Come to the End of Your Rope

Memory Verse

Be strong __*in the*__ __*Lord*__ and in the __*~~the~~ strength*__ of his __*might*__.

Ephesians 6:10

I heard the door shut behind me, and my heart sank.

I grabbed the doorknob and tried to turn it, but this only confirmed my reason to panic. I was locked out of the house. And while that was a problem, the real problem was what was locked *inside* the house.

I had stepped into the garage to feed the dog, leaving our newborn baby girl asleep in the living room. Since I didn't expect to stay in the garage long, I also left all means of communication in the living room.

So to recap, my baby, my phone, and my dog were all *inside* the house. I was the only one *not* inside the house.

My heart raced as I considered my options. As a Christian, I knew I should pray. So I did. I frantically asked God to help me. Then I said "Amen," opened my eyes, and grabbed a hammer.

It seemed like a good idea. With my hammer in hand, I swung as hard as I could at the glass-paned door, and … nothing. It turned out it wasn't a glass-paned door after all. Instead, since we lived in a city prone to hurricanes, it was another kind of material that proved to be hurricane-proof and hammer-proof.

Hmm. I needed a new plan.

My eye fell on the garage window, so I climbed out of it. It didn't lead me inside the house, but at least I was going somewhere. Somewhere with more windows. And maybe one would break when I hit it with the hammer.

I chose the window that I believed would make the least amount of mess, and I hit it with all my might. This time, it did break. But it turned out this window was double paned. The more I thought about it, I wasn't even sure I could squeeze through if, in fact, I did break through both sheets of glass.

Out of options and now wet and cold (did I mention it was raining?), I crawled back into the garage to regroup.

As I realized my best effort had landed me right back where I started, I decided to pray again. But this time was different. This time, when I told God my needs and asked Him for help, I didn't have a predetermined plan. This time, I asked Him to move and my only option was to expect that He would.

When I opened my eyes from this prayer, I put down my hammer. With my hands and heart available, I spotted a flat-head screwdriver. In a matter of seconds, I used the screwdriver to pop open the locked door. I stepped back inside the house to find the baby still sleeping right where I had left her. The dog was also still sleeping.

God's way was so much better than mine.

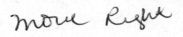

As we learn how to rely on our Savior, I want you to consider how you would handle the following situation. You are driving down the road and see a flashing yellow sign that reads "Left lane closed ahead." Use the space below to write what you would do.

move Right

You may have written that you would turn on the blinker and merge into the right lane. Maybe you said you would slow your speed. Whatever you wrote, you likely said you would engage in some kind of action. Based on what the sign said, you expected a lane to be closed and you altered your actions based on what you expected to happen down the road.

I think we sometimes ask God to help us or lead us but then, as I did in the garage, we get up from our knees and set off to figure things out alone. We acknowledge God, but we don't rely on Him. But as I learned in the garage that night, today we will see that God's will is always better than our ways and that the only way to live clothed in strength and dignity is to rely on Him.

DIGGING DEEPER

Turn in your Bible to John 6, and read verses 5–11.

What did Jesus give the crowd?

bread

Now read John 6:33–35. What did Jesus offer the crowd?

Himself

As John 6 begins, we see Jesus in front of a hungry crowd. They had traveled to see Him but had brought nothing to sustain them physically, so Jesus took the opportunity to perform one of His best-known miracles. He sat thousands of people down on a hillside, and with just five loaves of bread and two fish, He filled their bellies.

But the very next day, Jesus' second encounter with this crowd proved much different from the first. On the first day, Jesus multiplied the bread, everyone ate their fill, and Jesus was a crowd favorite. The next day, He shifted the focus from earth to eternity, from full bellies to satisfied souls … but this time, it wasn't what the crowd was looking for.

Yes, they were looking for the Messiah. Just after the miracle, they had even proclaimed, "This is indeed the Prophet who is to come into the world!" (v. 14). But in this second exchange, Jesus exposed a hidden motive.

Read John 6:26. According to Jesus, why was the crowd seeking Him?

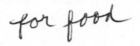

for food

The crowd came *to* Jesus, but they didn't come *for* Him. They sought Him with earthly gain in mind, not eternal glory. It was the same crowd in front of the same Jesus, but when offered the bread of life, they turned away (v. 66). His teaching about the bread of life wasn't easy to understand, and they didn't see any immediate satisfaction. Consequently, they didn't want it.

Sometimes I think we approach God and say things like "I need Your provision" or even "I *expect* Your provision." But then we lift our heads from prayer and set off to work out our own will instead of believing that God will lead us His way.

It could be that we treat Jesus the same way the crowd did that day. We don't come to Him to receive His will—instead, we desire Him to work things out our way. While our actions may suggest we're relying on the Lord, in order to truly surrender, to truly rely on our Savior instead of ourselves, we have to empty ourselves of our own will and fully accept God's ways.

That is the difference between counterfeit strength and the real thing. The dictionary defines *counterfeit* as "made in exact imitation of something valuable or important with the intention to deceive or defraud."[1] Based on this definition, answer these questions:

What kind of imitation is a counterfeit? *exact*

What is the purpose of a counterfeit? *to deceive or defraud*

It's like the girl on the magazine cover I saw one day. As I waited to check out at the local grocery store, I skimmed the magazine covers. Perfect images graced most of them. It was something I expected. Everybody knows they airbrush. One particular magazine displayed a famous singer. She looked flawless as she showed off her new swimsuit line.

At first glance, she looked like a girl standing much as I would on a normal day. As I inspected what looked so natural, I uncovered her secret. What looked so effortless wasn't. She was posing. The way she stood was meant to look natural, but that natural appearance took a lot of work.

When I got home, I tried to recreate her stance. I pulled my knee up, put a hand on my hip, and lowered one shoulder, all the while trying to keep my other arm behind my hip and push that shoulder back. As you can imagine, it was a bit of a disaster. And, might I add, it hurt! The pose was uncomfortable, and if I had tried to hold it for any amount of time, I might have done harm that would have been hard to undo.

Counterfeits are everywhere, and we have to be on the lookout for them. There are two sure indicators of a counterfeit:

First, *a counterfeit can't withstand the test of time.* I once owned a purse that was a counterfeit. Its likeness to the real thing was uncanny. While I wasn't an expert, I couldn't spot even one difference between the purse I carried and the real thing, which other people paid a hefty price for … until I had used it for a few weeks. My purse began to fray. The seams unraveled and the zipper started getting stuck. My new purse couldn't handle my lifestyle. Just like that purse and the pose I tried to recreate, counterfeit strength and dignity can't handle the load of our everyday lives. They will wear out.

Second, *a counterfeit costs a lot less.* It costs less because it's worth less. The value of a counterfeit doesn't compare to the real thing. So while a low price tag might be enticing, it can also signal something worthless. Jesus told His disciples the cost of following Him. He said, "If you try to hang on to your life, you will lose it. But if you give up your life for my sake, you will save it" (Luke 9:24 NLT). To live in Christ, to truly keep our lives safe and sound, we have to lose them for His sake.

When we come to the end of ourselves, we often encounter our breaking point, and our breaking point can become our boasting point.

As long as we rely on our own strength, we will be forced to carry our burdens on our own shoulders. We might swing hammers at all of life's windows, trying with all our might to break through to a solution. When we do, we will likely end up just as I did: wet, cold, and out of options.

If you find yourself in that place today, I have good news for you. When we come to the end of ourselves, we often encounter our breaking point, and our breaking point can become our boasting point—the point at which we can finally understand what Paul meant when he said, "I will boast all the more gladly of my weaknesses.... For when I am weak, then I am strong" (2 Cor. 12:9–10).

When our own strength falls short and we have nowhere else to turn, we can finally be strengthened by the Lord.

WORK IT OUT

> ✺ **To smile without fear of the future, I need to rely on my Savior instead of myself.** ✺

Think back to a time when you posed in counterfeit strength and dignity. What happened in your life when this counterfeit began to wear out?

As you consider surrendering your ways to God's will, I want to share with you a short prayer that I say as I seek to rely on my Savior instead of myself. Each time I pray this, I'm reminded that none of this is about me. It is all about God—His strength, His plan, and His glory. Feel free to pray this prayer or use it to help you write your own.

Dear God,
I can't ... but You can.
I don't have this ... but You've got this.
And You are in me.

Day 5

People Who Did the Impossible

Memory Verse

Be _strong_ in _the_ _Lord_
and in the _strength_ of his _might_.

Ephesians 6:10

To begin today's time, read Hebrews 11.

We've studied all week about relying on Jesus and His strength instead of our own. But I think we can sometimes talk about God's strength and still have trouble trusting it. Since we don't always notice the display of God's power, and since we more commonly notice earthly power, I think it's important to slow down and consider what we're talking about.

The Bible records story after story of regular people who did impossible things because of the power of God working in them, through them, and all around them. Hebrews 11 has been called the Hall of Faith chapter. It lists people throughout Bible history who "by faith" accomplished amazing things because they relied on God's strength and believed that with Him nothing is impossible. Verse 32 alone lists several of those names.

Look up Hebrews 11:32, and record the names it mentions:

On this list we see Gideon, a man who called himself the least member of the weakest clan in his tribe yet who with God's strength conquered the nation of Midian with only three hundred men.

We also find the name of David, a shepherd boy who defeated a giant with only a slingshot and five stones, then went on to become king of Israel.

We read the name of Samuel, a boy who heard God's voice and answered His call at a time when it was rare to hear from the Lord.

And that's just one verse! The chapter goes on, building out the picture of what the people listed above accomplished:

> [32]What more shall I say? For time would fail me to tell of Gideon, Barak, Samson, Jephthah, of David and Samuel and the prophets—[33]who through faith conquered kingdoms, enforced justice, obtained promises, stopped the mouths of lions, [34]quenched the power of fire, escaped the edge of the sword, were made strong out of weakness, became mighty in war, put foreign armies to flight. (vv. 32–34)

Underline the words *through faith* in verse 33 and the words *were made strong out of weakness* in verse 34.

According to verse 34, what other things did the people on this list do as they were made strong out of their weakness?

If surrender swings open the door to God's strength, faith puts that strength on and walks through the door. I love how this chapter defines *faith*: "Faith is confidence in what we hope for and assurance about what we do not see" (v. 1 NIV).

Faith acts on God's strength. Through faith, these people were made strong out of weakness. Through faith, we too are made strong out of weakness. And through faith, we can live clothed with the strength and dignity of Jesus Christ.

WORK IT OUT

> ✄ **To smile without fear of the future, I need to rely on my Savior instead of myself.** ✄

One of my favorite songs right now is "Nobody" by the Christian band Casting Crowns. One line expresses the desire to be known simply as a blood-bought member of the family of God.[1] When I read name after name listed in Hebrews 11, I'm challenged to consider my willingness to surrender my strength in order to be strong in the Lord and in His mighty power.

As we close this week, take a few minutes to be honest about where you are on this matter. What do you need to do differently in order to rely on your Savior instead of yourself? Does any part of this make you hesitate? Why do you think that is?

Use this space to journal about what God has revealed to you this week.

Through faith, we too are made strong out of weakness.

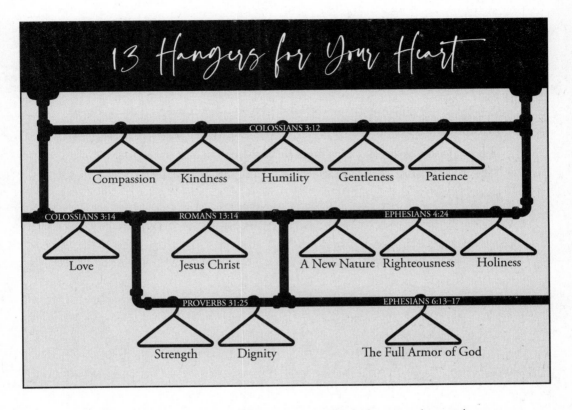

13 Hangers for Your Heart

COLOSSIANS 3:12 — Compassion · Kindness · Humility · Gentleness · Patience

COLOSSIANS 3:14 — Love · **ROMANS 13:14** — Jesus Christ · **EPHESIANS 4:24** — A New Nature · Righteousness · Holiness

PROVERBS 31:25 — Strength · Dignity · **EPHESIANS 6:13–17** — The Full Armor of God

"As God's chosen people, holy and dearly loved, clothe yourselves with compassion, kindness, humility, gentleness and patience." (Col. 3:12 NIV)

"Above all, clothe yourselves with love, which binds us all together in perfect harmony." (Col. 3:14 NLT)

"Put on the Lord Jesus Christ, and make no plans to satisfy the fleshly desires." (Rom. 13:14 HCSB)

"Put on your new nature, created to be like God—truly righteous and holy." (Eph. 4:24 NLT)

"Strength and dignity are her clothing, and she smiles at the future." (Prov. 31:25 NASB)

"Put on the full armor of God, so that when the day of evil comes, you may be able to stand your ground, and after you have done everything, to stand. Stand firm then, with the belt of truth buckled around your waist, with the breastplate of righteousness in place, and with your feet fitted with the readiness that comes from the gospel of peace. In addition to all this, take up the shield of faith, with which you can extinguish all the flaming arrows of the evil one. Take the helmet of salvation and the sword of the Spirit, which is the word of God." (Eph. 6:13–17 NIV)

Video Session 4:
Her Heart's Preparation

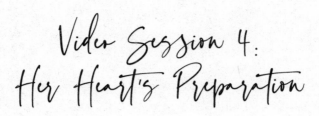

Watch video session 4, and use this space to write notes or record insights.

_____

_____

_____

_____

_____

_____

_____

_____

_____

_____

_____

_____

_____

_____

_____

_____

_____

_____

_____

_____

_____

_____

Week 4

Her Heart's Pursuit: Living Directed

Memory Verse

Love bears all things, believes all things,
hopes all things, endures all things.

1 Corinthians 13:7

Introduction

No one could have predicted what had just transpired.

On a hot summer evening, we had lined our chairs up next to the fence. Eager little boys darted onto the baseball field with their caps low and gloves in hand. It was a typical night at the ballpark. At least for a moment.

As usual I tried to keep one eye on the field and the other eye on the rest of my kids, who always found something interesting to do. Some played tag with friends. Others made handprints in the dirt. Every now and then, someone tried to climb the big tree by the concession stand.

On this night, though, a previously unnoticed attraction captured my toddler's attention. My youngest son spotted a pipe that emerged from the ground. Oh, the questions that must have swarmed through his mind! *Where is this pipe coming from? What might be inside? What is it for? What does it do? Why is it here?*

As his thoughts swirled, he inched closer and closer to the pipe. The opening at the top was about the size of a quarter. As he drew near to the mysterious pipe, something wonderful happened, at least for him. He found a knob. A knob! Right next to the pipe! It doesn't get any better than that.

With both of my eyes on the field, my youngest boy took his chance. He turned the knob … and turned the baseball field into a water park.

Without warning, a geyser of water burst forth from the pipe. The parents who had been lined up by the fence became recipients of a surprise summer shower. My mama instincts kicked in, and I stopped the waterspout before we all got too drenched. It ended up being more refreshing than soaking.

And now we know to keep an eye out for any pipes at the ballpark.

Day 1

Chasing Happy

Memory Verse

Love bears all things, believes all things, hopes all things, endures all things.

1 Corinthians 13:7

If you are, like me, a type-A girl who has been waiting three whole weeks of this study to actually *do* something, congratulations, friend—this is your week! We finally made it to the section about our actions. It's time to put our hearts in motion. But before we get into it, let's not forget all the work we've done through the last three weeks.

When we position and prepare our hearts to embrace God's plans, our actions become much like the geyser my son created at the baseball field that day. They gush out of our hearts and into the world around us. Those actions don't take much work. They're simply an overflow of hearts ready for God's purposes.

But if you are like me, you have to be careful. Because every day it can feel as though you're at a track-and-field meet and the starter's gun fires to signal the start of the new day of sprinting. We set our feet on the floor and sprint off into the day in pursuit of something, and if we are not careful, the culture, and even our own desires, will tell us what to pursue.

Most likely, we will chase Happy.

With our sights set on the finish line, whatever it may be, we can exhaust ourselves trying to reach Happy. We fix our eyes on personal goals or security, and everyone else gets left in the dust. But when we finally break through the ribbon to cheers and applause, hoping to breathe a deep sigh of relief, we realize there's one big problem with chasing Happy …

Once you get to Happy, Happy moves.

Almost a decade ago, my family and I bought a house in Texas. The uncertainty of Luke's job often left us wondering where we would live and how long we would stay in one place. For several years it felt like we moved every six months, so the stability of having a house near family spelled security and brought a smile to my heart.

When we walked through the front door, I knew God had picked this house for us. It was perfect. I loved the big windows in the main living space. I loved the nook where I envisioned my family eating meals together. I loved the trees I could see through the windows in almost every room. This home felt open and inviting. It was exactly what we had been looking for. A few weeks later, we bought the house and moved in.

Everything was perfect … until we decided the carpet must go. It was white carpet, and we had a lot of little kids. What had started as white was beginning to look more like a shade of brown. So we replaced the carpet.

A short time later, we overhauled the bathroom to make room for a tub to clean the kids who had made the carpet brown. After that we noticed how dingy the walls were getting. They certainly needed a new paint job.

We eventually painted walls, added rooms, replaced counters, and changed nearly every floor in the house … Happy moved.

Do you find yourself chasing after a picture of happiness that keeps moving? Describe your picture of happiness.

In the introduction to this study, I told you about the fateful night I slammed into a cement post because I was afraid of a thunderstorm looming in the distance. I've since learned that it isn't just threatening storms that can have us falling over things. Sometimes it can be rainbows. It might be the pursuit of future happiness in which we wrap up all our hopes. That pursuit can yield the same results as one motivated by fear. It can change us and rob us of confidence, security, and purpose in the present.

Happiness is not a bad thing, and to live directed by God's leading does not mean we will be unhappy. In fact, according to the Bible, godly pursuits and happiness intersect.

> Blessed are the people who know the festal shout,
>   who walk, O LORD, in the light of your face,
> who exult in your name all the day
>   and in your righteousness are exalted. (Ps. 89:15–16)

The Hebrew word translated "blessed" in verse 15 is sometimes translated "happy" and is often accompanied by an exclamation point. This passage begins with the phrase "Blessed are the people who," which is followed by four things that describe these people who are blessed.

List those four things here:

First, it says that people who are blessed "know the festal shout." God's Word Translation describes those who know the festal shout as "the people who know how to praise you." Next, the ESV says blessed people walk "in the light of [God's] face." Then these verses describe happy and blessed people as those who "find joy in [God's] name all day long" (GW).[1] Finally, the passage says that people who are blessed are exalted in God's righteousness.

I don't know if you caught it, but this is what we've been doing for the last three weeks: In week 1, we learned to remain in the presence of God, much like how Psalm 89:15 says blessed people walk in the light of His face. In week 2, we learned how the fear of the LORD fuels worship of Him. People who are blessed practice praising God. Last week, we read about how strength is found in the name of the Lord, and Psalm 89:16 says blessed people find joy in the name of the Lord all day long.

The world gives us opinions on where to find happiness, but those pursuits are very different from the ones we find in Proverbs 31. The happiness the world offers is fleeting and momentary and will never satisfy our souls. To pursue true happiness, we must first pursue God.

The woman who smiles without fear is busy, but she is not aimless in her busyness.

I used to read about the Proverbs 31 woman and think these verses weren't about action at all. I felt so strongly about the heart *behind* her actions that I almost dismissed her actions entirely. But the Bible does not disconnect our actions from our faith. Instead, much like the story about my son and the waterspout, the Bible says our actions are directly related to our hearts.

Our actions reveal the position of our hearts. We are not saved by works, and we are not secure because of works. However, salvation and security in Christ cannot help but produce good works within us that glorify our Father in heaven (see Matt. 5:16; James 2:18).

Our friend in Proverbs 31 refuses to chase the world's definition of Happy. This week, we will examine several of her pursuits. To get started, read Proverbs 31:13–16 and fill in the following blanks:

She seeks _____.

She brings _____.

She provides _____ and portions _____.

She considers _____.

The woman who smiles without fear is busy, but she is not aimless in her busyness. Her pursuits are directed not toward selfish or earthly ambitions but toward the things that bring true happiness and eternal satisfaction.

DIGGING IN

Read the verse below, and underline four things we are told to pursue:

> Flee youthful passions and pursue righteousness, faith, love, and peace, along
> with those who call on the Lord from a pure heart. (2 Tim. 2:22)

Before telling us what to pursue, this verse says we should do something else first. What is it?

The Greek word translated "youthful" is used only one time (here) in the New Testament. It means "peculiar to the age of youth."[2] Compare this to what we read here:

> When I was a child, I spoke like a child, I thought like a child, I reasoned like
> a child. When I became a man, I gave up childish ways. (1 Cor. 13:11)

Underline the three things that Paul, the writer of this verse, did in a childish way when he was young.

What are some characteristics of how a child speaks, thinks, and reasons?

When we are young, our pursuits tend to revolve around our desires. They are often characterized by self-indulgence and shortsightedness. We want what makes us feel good, and we seek what satisfies us immediately. Wisdom and reason are often still developing, and we have difficulty seeing beyond what is right in front of us. Therefore, we chase Happy.

    To become women who smile without fear, we must decide to put aside our childish pursuits and run not after temporary gains and fleeting feel-good moments but after righteousness, faith, love, and peace.

    Let's look at 2 Timothy 2:22 again, but this time, let's read it in the Amplified Bible:

> Shun youthful lusts *and* flee from them, and aim at *and* pursue righteousness (all that is virtuous and good, right living, conformity to the will of God in thought, word, and deed); [and aim at and pursue] faith, love, [and] peace (harmony and concord with others) in fellowship with all [Christians], who call upon the Lord out of a pure heart. (AMPC)

Based on what you read in this verse, define *righteousness*.

Define *peace*.

How does this verse say we are to aim at and pursue righteousness, faith, love, and peace?

    We can exhaust ourselves on the chase for the world's definition of Happy. That chase will ultimately leave us only dissatisfied and disappointed. Or we can pursue happiness as it is defined in God's Word. That pursuit will lead us where we want to go: to love, peace, and all that is good.

WORK IT OUT

Think through a typical day in your life. Where do you go? Who do you talk to? What do you do?

After you answer these questions, consider *why* you do all those things. Whether you have made an intentional decision or not, everything you do is likely aimed at something. What is your ultimate goal for where you go, what you do, and who you engage with?

What does your answer say about your current pursuit? Are you chasing Happy, or are you pursuing righteousness, faith, love, and peace?

Target Practice

Memory Verse

Love _____ all things, believes all things, hopes all things, endures all things.

1 Corinthians 13:7

Before so many great advancements in technology, sailors depended on the lighthouse for direction and safety. On a dark, stormy night, one beam of light from shore could spark hope in the heart of a lonely man at sea.

Imagine a captain on the ocean waves. His white knuckles grip the wheel of the ship as the waves crash against the side of his boat and he sweats, trying to keep her afloat. He works to keep calm for his crew, but on the inside, he wonders if they will pull through.

Then a light pierces the blanket of darkness, signaling a safe place ahead. His eyes no longer linger on the rough seas surrounding him. He can fasten his eyes on the light—the hope in the midst of the storm.

The lighthouse braves the same storm as do those at sea. The difference is where she stands. Her feet sink deep into solid ground. Her unique shape and stable body reduce the effects of the strong winds. The maker of this lighthouse built her for a storm such as this, so she stands. She stands tall. She stands firm. And she shines.

Yesterday we exposed the place where our pursuits can veer off track. We can exhaust our-selves chasing Happy and never really catch up with it. Today let's draw a target at which all our pursuits can be aimed. Yesterday we read four things to pursue in 2 Timothy 2:22—righteousness, faith, love, and peace. For our purposes, we're going to narrow that list down to one.

Draw a line to match each verse below to what it says about love.

Colossians 3:14	casts out fear
1 John 4:18	is the greatest of virtues
1 Corinthians 13:13	binds everything together in harmony
Matthew 22:36–40	is the greatest commandment
John 13:35	how the world will know us

Love identifies us and unites us. It expels fear and compels us. These five references don't cover all of what the Bible has to say about love, of course, but they are enough to bring us to our fourth step to smiling without fear of the future:

> ❧ **To smile without fear of the future, I need to pursue love.** ❧

With love so central to our goal, it's vital that we have an accurate definition of it. How do you define love?

Our definition of love is often influenced by the earthly love we've experienced. In a world where love and acceptance are so often performance based, it seems love must be earned—and once earned, it must be kept. On earth, love is often based on your status or what you have to offer. And if you have nothing, you receive nothing. But the love that the Bible teaches isn't the same as the love that the world produces. Let's take another look at a few of the verses referenced above, beginning with 1 John 4:18: "There is no fear in love, but perfect love casts out fear."

This verse doesn't say that any kind of love casts out fear. It says that only "perfect love" drives out fear. Another verse in the same chapter defines this perfect love. It says, "God is love" (v. 16).

God's love is far different from human love. Our love is flawed, conditional, and limited. God's love spares us from spiritual death and leads us into eternal life. The perfect love we seek to pursue starts with God and His love. To pursue love is to pursue God.

When we receive God's love, it completes us and enables us to share His love with others. The opposite of fear is love—God's perfect love.

Now that we know God's love is not the same as earthly love, we can dive deeper into what God's love is.

While reading through the verses about love, you read 1 Corinthians 13:13. This verse concludes a chapter in the Bible that provides us with a more detailed description of love. Here's a portion of it:

> Love is patient and kind; love does not envy or boast; it is not arrogant or rude. It does not insist on its own way; it is not irritable or resentful; it does not rejoice at wrongdoing, but rejoices with the truth. Love bears all things, believes all things, hopes all things, endures all things. (vv. 4–7)

These four verses are packed with indicators of love. Write some of the words that describe love. Which is most difficult for you to put into practice?

DIGGING IN

The description of love in 1 Corinthians 13:4–7 will be the definition we use as we learn to pursue love. The bookends of this definition of love are patience and endurance. These two Greek words carry similar meanings. The word translated "patient" is *makrothymeō*, which means "to be of a long spirit" or "to not lose heart." It can refer to patiently persevering in times of trouble or being slow to anger when bearing the offenses of others.[1]

The Greek word for "endures" is *hypomenō* and means "to remain, i.e., abide, not recede or flee."[2] Does that remind you of something? Just as we learned about remaining in Christ during week 1, as we study how to pursue love we will find that this pursuit can be realized only as we *remain* in Christ.

Patience and endurance are tucked into almost everything the Proverbs 31 woman does. Let's dig deeper into her flurry of activity to find them.

Consider Proverbs 31:13: "She selects wool and flax and works with eager hands" (NIV). This verse describes the beginning of a process. Wool and flax were common products in the ancient world and were harvested and modified to produce textiles. The process required several steps that involved physical exertion and time. The flax stalks had to be gathered, steeped in water, and spread out to dry. These are ordinary tasks, yet we read about how the woman in Proverbs 31 approaches them "with eager hands."

List some of your common, ordinary tasks.

What kind of attitude do you typically approach these tasks with?

In the mundane routine of everyday life, the heart of this woman remains eager and willing. Several verses in Proverbs 31 reveal why she may have worked with such eagerness. Read the verses below, and write down what becomes of the wool and flax she selects:

Proverbs 31:21 ⟶

Proverbs 31:22 •————►

Proverbs 31:24 •————►

She approaches her tasks expectantly. Her hands are eager because she anticipates what will become of her work and who will be blessed by it. Read these three verses again. This time, record who benefits from her work:

Proverbs 31:21 •————►

Proverbs 31:22 •————►

Proverbs 31:24 •————►

Verse 20 adds another group of people who benefit from her eager hands. The poor and needy are also served as her work produces an overflow of abundance that gives her the ability to share.

We all have our own processes that play out in the rhythms of our everyday lives. If we're not careful, the processes of our daily lives can become robotic. We don't approach them with eager hands. Instead, we do them with disconnected hands. We show up in body but not in spirit. Often this zombie-like existence is connected to a lack of purpose. We don't do our tasks with eagerness because we don't see or believe in the result of what we are doing.

For example, I used to get grumpy about going to the grocery store. It was a regular task that I just didn't enjoy doing. It wasn't until God led me to view this task as a part of a bigger process that my heart began to change. I came to understand that the trip to the grocery store allowed me the blessing of providing food for my family. The food I provided for my family helped them grow and be healthy. As God opened my eyes to the end result of this ordinary task, my attitude shifted. I no longer approached it grudgingly; instead, I felt thankful.

Look back at your list of ordinary tasks. What larger process is each task a part of?

The woman in Proverbs 31 engages in typical daily tasks with eager hands because she works with the end in mind. In doing so, her work blesses her household and her community—and even she herself is blessed by her work.

I don't want you to get discouraged by this. Certainly we all have days when we're just not feeling it. This isn't meant to condemn us or set an impossible standard. Instead, it's meant to free us to fully invest in the assignments right in front of us.

What parts of your current processes have you decided are insignificant or lacking purpose? How might a change in how you approach your tasks bless the people you influence?

Possibly the most exciting result of her work is recorded in Proverbs 31:18: "She sees that her trading is profitable, and her lamp does not go out at night" (NIV).

Some translations replace *trading* with *merchandise*.[3] The word seems to communicate profitability beyond her trading. It may encompass the entirety of her work, implying that she evaluates *all* she does and perceives it is profitable. She's looking for a profit—not necessarily a monetary profit but something of gain. She evaluates her work to determine whether it is beneficial to her household and others she cares for. She looks for fruit.

Twice in Proverbs 31:10–31, we read about the fruit this woman produces. In verse 16 she invests the fruit of her hands in a vineyard that will yield more gain. In verse 31 she receives the fruit of her hands. In other words, she reaps what she has sown.

Your daily pursuits likely do not include selecting wool and flax, and you may not spin fibers into bed coverings or sashes. But whatever your catalog of activity includes, you can be intentional about producing gain—abundance to be enjoyed by your household and all those under your influence. Let's also remember what we learned about producing fruit in week 1—to produce fruit, we must remain connected to Jesus.

As you consider the processes you are currently living out, would you say your work is producing fruit? Why or why not?

Don't get discouraged by the last part of Proverbs 31:18. It isn't telling us we need to stay up all night (and all God's girls said "Amen!"). The last sentence is actually full of promise.

In the ancient world, a lamp that did not go out at night would bring to mind a few different ideas. First, it could represent diligence in work. It could also be considered a sign of life or enduring prosperity. In contrast to a lamp that does not go out, the book of Proverbs refers to the lamp of the wicked that is snuffed out (see 13:9 NIV; 24:20 NIV).[4]

A lamp that doesn't go out could also depict hope in the darkness of difficult circumstances.[5] The woman in Proverbs 31 does not smile without fear because she never has anything to fear. Instead, she smiles because no matter what she faces, she pursues love. "Love bears all things, believes all things, hopes all things, endures all things" (1 Cor. 13:7). Therefore, much like a lighthouse, even at night her lamp does not go out. Her hope does not fade. Her endurance does not waver. Whether her profit is seen or not yet realized, she pursues love.

The opposite of fear is love—God's perfect love.

You may be in a part of your process where your work has not yet revealed a profit, at least not one you can see. You may be raising a child who has walked away from the truth. You may have a loved one who is physically or spiritually sick. In moments like these, we cannot always see the profit in the process. Today let me encourage you to keep pursuing love. The pursuit of love requires patience with the process.

As we read through the actions of the Proverbs 31 woman this week, I want to encourage you to resist the urge to compare your present reality with what you read. These verses are not meant to catalog one day's worth of production in this woman's life. Some scholars suggest that this chapter is not designed to describe one actual woman but instead may be a combination of the attributes of many women.[6] At the very least, these verses represent a lifelong process of pursuing love.

WORK IT OUT

> ❧ **To smile without fear of the future, I need to pursue love.** ❧

Each day this week, I want us to make 1 Corinthians 13:4–7 a personal prayer. Below is an example. Feel free to pray this prayer or write one of your own.

> Dear Jesus, help me today to be patient and kind. Help me not to be jealous. I don't want to brag or be arrogant. Lord, help me not act rude. Help me not insist on my own way or be irritable or resentful. I do not want to rejoice at wrongdoing, but help me rejoice with the truth. Jesus, today help me bear all things, believe all things, hope all things, and endure all things. Amen.

As you pray this, circle any word or phrase that stands out or that you feel prompted to focus on. After you have prayed this prayer, ask God to show you His goals and purposes for your ordinary daily tasks. Ask Him to help you see them through His eyes. Use the space below to journal about what God shows you.

_____

_____

_____

_____

To smile without fear of the future, I need to pursue love.

Three Ways to Pursue Love

Memory Verse

Love _____ all things, _____
all things, hopes all things, endures all things.
1 Corinthians 13:7

I'm notorious for walking through the grocery store without a list.

Sometimes I'll jot down a few items I absolutely cannot forget—coffee, for instance—but my scribbled notes usually end up stuffed deep inside the pit of my purse, so I just wing it as I walk up and down the aisles.

Consequently, I almost always forget something.

I start with a purpose. I mean, before I step through those sliding doors, I definitely know what I've come to get. I catalog the dishes I want to cook that week and sort through a list of ingredients I'll need. (Before we pull out our measuring sticks again, don't go getting ideas of any made-from-scratch, take-all-day-to-make dinners. I once said it this way: I cook stuff that tastes good and takes no talent or time.)

But back to the grocery store … because I either neglect to make a list or forget to consult it, I often end up in the kitchen, ready to cook yet missing one key ingredient. That's when I search the internet for a worthy substitute I might have on hand or I text my mother-in-law to see if she might have my missing ingredient in her cabinet.

In the grocery store, as in life, it's good to have a plan. Without a plan, we wander aimlessly and keep our fingers crossed that we'll end up with everything we need to achieve the desired result.

I don't know whether the words I'm about to utter will be the most beautiful words you've read in the last four weeks or if they'll send you running. Eek! Are you ready?

Today we're going to make a list.

Yes! Do your happy dance or sing your celebration song (or take some deep breaths and continue reading only after you recover), because this is happening. Today you will learn a list of ingredients, so to speak, that will help you pursue love.

The actions of the woman in Proverbs 31 flow from a heart that knows God's love and shows it to others. This love produces a pattern of unselfish actions rooted in practices that we too can apply.

The work that the woman in Proverbs 31 approaches with eager hands is not easy or insignificant. It is difficult work that combines clear direction with intentional pursuit. It is work that she knows will demand physical, emotional, and spiritual strength. But it is worth it.

Let's review our definition of love:

> Love is patient and kind; love does not envy or boast; it is not arrogant or rude. It does not insist on its own way; it is not irritable or resentful; it does not rejoice at wrongdoing, but rejoices with the truth. Love bears all things, believes all things, hopes all things, endures all things. (1 Cor. 13:4–7)

If something in these verses jumped out at you today, record that here.

Now let's get to that list.

DIGGING IN

To help us set about our work vigorously and to intentionally pursue love in our everyday assignments, we can practice three things:

1. Work with consistency.
2. Work hard.
3. Work without complaining.

This list will be the guide you use to make your list in the "Work It Out" section of today's study. The woman in Proverbs 31 gives us an example of each item on our list. Let's take a deeper look at how she pursues love.

First, *the woman in Proverbs 31 works with consistency*. "She is like the ships of the merchant; she brings her food from afar" (v. 14).

In the ancient world, merchant ships operated with consistency and regularity. They brought with them treasure and "a continual supply of abundance."[1] When this verse compares the woman to a merchant ship, it paints a picture of a woman who works with consistency and excellence. She shows up every day to tackle the tasks at hand, bringing her best.

Consistency can be one of the most difficult parts of an assignment. Consistency requires commitment. It requires us to show up when we feel like it and when we don't. And not just show up but show up with a heart ready to love and serve.

What are some of the most difficult things for you to remain consistent in? Why are they difficult?

Consistency is closely related to patience and endurance. It's much easier to continue in a task when it produces results. When we exercise and eat right, we want to see our pants size decrease. When we clean the house, we want someone to tell us how great it looks. When we go above and beyond what is expected of us at work, we want the employee-of-the-month parking space and maybe a trophy. But the verses about the Proverbs 31 woman don't emphasize immediate results. Instead, they point to patient repetition.

The further we get into this, the more obvious it becomes that we cannot pursue love in our own strength. Remember what we talked about yesterday—to pursue love is to pursue God. We love because He first loved us (1 John 4:19). You may even need to go back to week 1. Reread John 15:1–10, and remind yourself what it takes to produce this kind of fruit.

To grow in strength, we must do things that require strength.

Second, *she works hard.* "She rises while it is yet night and provides food for her household and portions for her maidens" (Prov. 31:15).

For those of us who are not morning people, this verse is one we'd like to skip over. The woman in Proverbs 31 rises while it is still night for a reason. This woman does what needs to be done no matter what it costs her. She works diligently. If she has to get up earlier than everyone else, she does. If it's still night, so be it. She doesn't choose her pursuits based on convenience. It actually seems quite the opposite—she chooses to pursue hard things.

The verse that follows gives more details about this hard work: "With the fruit of her hands she plants a vineyard" (v. 16). Planting a vineyard in her day wasn't quite the same as planting flowers in front of our houses. Planting a vineyard would have been hard physical work with many steps. She would first have had to clear the field of stones. She and her helpers may have built a wall around the field before she dug the winepress. She may have even built a watchtower in the field (see Isa. 5:1–2; Mark 12:1). The work referred to in these verses wasn't easy.

To grow in strength, we must do things that require strength.

Comparing her actions to the definition of love from 1 Corinthians 13, we see a woman who is not self-seeking. She does not shy away from difficult tasks so that she may indulge her own comforts or desires. She does not boast about what she has or envy what someone else has. Instead, she humbly works hard, investing the fruit of her labor for the sake of others.

What work are you avoiding because it seems too difficult? Who might benefit from your willingness to work hard?

Third on our list, *the Proverbs 31 woman pursues love by working without complaining.* "She opens her mouth with wisdom, and the teaching of kindness is on her tongue" (v. 26). Underline the two things that come out of her mouth.

The passage of Proverbs 31:10–31 is a form of poetry called an acrostic. Each verse begins with a successive letter of the Hebrew alphabet. Writers did this for the sake of memorization, but the use of an acrostic could also imply comprehensiveness.[2] The writer could have been saying that this catalog of her character was complete from *A* to *Z*, encompassing every virtue and skill.

This brings us to verse 26. In the middle of all her doing, this verse includes what she is *saying.* Love influences both her works and her words.[3] The Hebrew word translated "kindness" in verse 26 is *hesed*, and it is the same word that is used to describe God's steadfast love for His people.[4]

First Corinthians 13:4–7 gives several options of things that could come out of our mouths. We could boast or be rude. We could insist on our own way or speak out of frustration. We could even celebrate unrighteousness. But love does not, and neither does the woman in Proverbs 31. Look up the four scriptures below, and fill in the blanks with what they teach us about how we should use our words.

	DO SPEAK	DO NOT SPEAK
Ephesians 4:29		
Ephesians 5:4		
Colossians 4:6		
1 Thessalonians 5:11		

The words of the Proverbs 31 woman can be trusted. She's so wise that even her words produce profit. They are beneficial to the listener and useful so that whoever hears them may be complete and equipped.

Notice the connection between the tongue and the heart: "The tongue of the righteous is choice silver; the heart of the wicked is of little worth" (Prov. 10:20).

Jesus' words make it so clear: "The mouth speaks what the heart is full of" (Luke 6:45 GNT[5]).

In case I haven't said it enough, let me say it one more time: we cannot do this on our own. To smile without fear of the future, we need to pursue love. To pursue love, we must remain connected to the Vine. We must revere God. We must rely on our Savior. In all our pursuing, we cannot forget the first three steps of this journey: God is love. Jesus is the wisdom of God. To pursue love, we must pursue God.

WORK IT OUT

> ✄ **To smile without fear of the future, I need to pursue love.** ✄

Pray 1 Corinthians 13:4–7:

> Dear Jesus, help me today to be patient and kind. Help me not to be jealous. I don't want to brag or be arrogant. Lord, help me not act rude. Help me not insist on my own way or be irritable or resentful. I do not want to rejoice at wrongdoing, so help me rejoice with the truth. Jesus, today help me bear all things, believe all things, hope all things, and endure all things. Amen.

Turn to the "Love Target" resource at the end of this week's study. On the arrows, write down the processes of your daily life. You might write your job, your children's names, a ministry project, or even a process you'd like to begin but haven't started yet. After you fill in your arrows (and you don't have to fill in every one), look below for three ways to pursue love:

1. Work with consistency.
2. Work hard.
3. Work without complaining.

Now it's time to make your own list. Take what you wrote on the arrows, and consider how you can work with consistency, work hard, and work without complaining in the midst of your daily life. Then write down specific things you will do to pursue love in your daily processes.

_____

_____

_____

_____

_____

_____

_____

_____

_____

_____

_____

_____

_____

_____

_____

_____

_____

_____

_____

Day 4

Who Will Think of Me?

Memory Verse

Love _____ all things, _____ all

things, _____ all things, endures all things.

1 Corinthians 13:7

I scurried about, packing myself, my kids, and my husband. The weeklong adventure ahead of us would be fun—if only we could get there. And, of course, one of the kids turned up sick the day before we left.

I tried to comfort my patient and keep his siblings from meddling too much with his germs. All the while, the washing machine whirled and clothes piled up around me in semi-organized stacks.

Though I may have worn a smile on the outside, the conversation in my mind was erupting. *Why am I the only one in this house preparing to leave? Shouldn't someone else be a part of this process?* I grumbled. *Last time I checked, I wasn't the only one taking this trip. Why is it solely my responsibility to take care of every tiny detail?*

I continued to corral kids and shuffle clothes. No one else knew of my raging thoughts … until Luke walked through the door.

Completely unsuspecting, he bounded through the door, and when our sick child asked him for a cracker, Dad obliged. "Sure, buddy!" It was in this moment, as Luke reached for the cracker box, that the inner assault of my thoughts announced itself.

"No!" I basically shouted. "I'm in charge!"

I think it actually was as bad as it sounds. Imagine a fierce finger wag, and I'm sure you get the picture.

My outburst left my people stunned. Everyone within earshot froze. They all must have wondered what happened to me. After all, just one minute before, I had seemed pleasant and patient. In this minute, though, not so much.

I can almost always trace outbursts like this back to the conversation happening inside my head. It's a dialogue that elevates the importance of all that I'm doing and wonders why no one notices. I list one by one all that I've done and all I still have left to do. And as I feed those feelings, I grow increasingly frustrated. The next thing I know, rude words and actions spew out of my life.

As long as I have *me* on my mind, love will be hard to find. I know that, and based on the story above, you know I have experienced that. It's quite the opposite of how I want to live, but the source of the situation traces back to a question I silently ask: *If I don't think about me, who will?*

I don't know how this week has been for you. It may have been a hard one to absorb. While the pursuit of love brings purpose to our tasks, the overwhelming feeling of being unnoticed, overworked, and underappreciated casts a cloud over any hope we may have found. You may have scoured these Scriptures, looking for an indication that someone is caring for *her*. That someone is thinking of *her*. That someone is there for *her*.

You may have wondered, *In all her caring for others, who cares for her?* and *If I choose to pursue love, who will care for me?*

While it may appear that no one thinks of the woman in Proverbs 31, and while it may feel like no one thinks of you, that couldn't be further from the truth.

DIGGING IN

Read Psalm 8:4:

> What is man that you are mindful of him,
>   and the son of man that you care for him?

Underline the phrases that begin with "that you."

The *you* in this verse is God. The writer of Psalm 8, David, posed this question in wonderment at who God is and why He chooses to consider the human race at all. As he pondered this, David also noted two truths: *God thinks about us,* and *God cares for us.*

Because God thinks about us and cares for us, we don't have to do those things for ourselves. I don't have to have me on my mind, because God has me on His mind. Read those two truths again. Personalize them. Digest them. God thinks about *you.* God cares for *you.*

For years I fell victim to patterns of thought that led to frustration and outbursts. Patterns like this breed actions not of love but of the opposite. Remember the definition of the word *heart* from week 1. The heart is not merely the seat of emotions—the heart also informs everything we do, including how we think.

> Love is patient and kind; love does not envy or boast; it is not arrogant or
> rude. It does not insist on its own way; it is not irritable or resentful; it does
> not rejoice at wrongdoing, but rejoices with the truth. Love bears all things,
> believes all things, hopes all things, endures all things. (1 Cor. 13:4–7)

Sort the following word bank into the two columns to show the difference between what love is and what selfish thoughts produce.

> patience, envy, boasting, arrogance, rudeness, kindness, insisting on my own way, irritability, resentment

LOVE	SELFISH THOUGHTS

Thought patterns built on what we deserve provide fertile ground for rudeness, resentment, and irritability. Up to this point in our study, we've talked about our actions and the heart behind our actions, but there is one more important layer to the love we seek to pursue.

> Do not be conformed to this world, but be transformed by the renewal of
> your mind, that by testing you may discern what is the will of God, what is
> good and acceptable and perfect. (Rom. 12:2)

How does this verse say we are transformed?

What does it say is the result of the renewal of our minds?

To pursue love, we have to let God change the way we think. What happens in our minds is the starting line for what happens in our hearts, and what happens in our hearts is the catalyst for our pursuit of love.

Not only does Psalm 8 give us truth that allows us to take all *our* things off our minds, but it also gives us something to replace those thoughts with: our Lord.

After taking two verses to ponder the vastness of God's power and majesty, David leads us to consider who God is and what His rightful position in the universe is. But in Psalm 8 David did not just glance at God. Nor does he only pause to simply acknowledge God.

Read Psalm 8:3 and circle the word *look*: "When I look at your heavens, the work of your fingers, the moon and the stars, which you have set in place."

The Hebrew word for "look" in this verse is often translated "consider." Other definitions for this word are "to inspect" and "to look intently at."[1] I don't have to have me on my mind, because God has me on His. And because God has me on His mind, I am free to give my attention to who He is.

When your thoughts are focused on what you deserve or some wrong that someone has done to you, what would you say you are looking intently at?

When is the last time you determined to look intently at God? What was the result of fixing your eyes on Him?

When we let God control our minds, He works within us to create thanksgiving and causes us to thirst for His pursuits.

Consider Romans 8:6:

> Letting your sinful nature control your mind leads to death. But letting the
> Spirit control your mind leads to life and peace. (NLT)

In this verse, underline the outcome of letting your sinful nature control your mind. Circle the outcome of letting the Spirit control your mind.

As we move about our days, we weave life or death into its fibers. The whispers within determine whether our souls will be spoiled or satisfied every day. It's so easy to throw a really impressive pity party, especially when the service is high and the support is low or when we seek to do right and the ones around us don't seem to notice or care. We can make lists of all we deserve, all we've earned, and all the ways in which others have let us down … or we can give the Holy Spirit control over our hearts and minds.

I don't have to have me on my mind,
because God has me on His mind.

Let's not waste one more day smothered by deafening thoughts. Today let's start a new thought pattern—a pattern focused on pursuing love. One that is not resentful or irritable but one that invites the joy of the Lord to fill our souls as we think of Him.

And we don't have to wait until we feel like it to take this new path. We can let our actions lead our feelings. In their devotional book on Proverbs, Tim and Kathy Keller wrote,

> Modern people think feelings determine what we do and that it is hypocritical to act loving if they don't feel loving. Proverbs, however, tells us that our actions shape our feelings. So if you don't feel love for someone, don't let that stop you. Do the actions of love, and often the feelings follow.... So start doing the actions of love—take that path—and you will see your heart changing.[2]

Read Proverbs 31:30–31:

> Charm is deceptive, and beauty is fleeting;
>   but a woman who fears the LORD is to be praised.
> Honor her for all that her hands have done,
>   and let her works bring her praise at the city gate. (NIV)

Twice in the final verses about the Proverbs 31 woman the writer told of how she garners praise. She is to be praised because she fears the LORD and rewarded because of the work that flows from that. When we pursue love, we too will enjoy the rewards of living clothed with strength and dignity and smiling at the future. We will also store up for ourselves a future reward, a treasure in heaven that cannot be destroyed or stolen (see Matt. 6:19–20).

If you're like me, though, all this may still feel a little risky. To go all in—to aim our lives at love—can make us feel very vulnerable. It can feel like we're putting ourselves out there and setting ourselves up to be unnoticed, underappreciated, and unsupported. But remember, you don't have to have *you* on your mind, because God has you on His mind. That's why, if we are to pursue love, we must first know that we are loved. We must know God's love—and by *know*, I mean we daily experience God's love.

That's where I want to end today's time together, with our minds on God's love for us:

> Have this mind among yourselves, which is yours in Christ Jesus, who, though he was in the form of God, did not count equality with God a thing to be grasped, but emptied himself, by taking the form of a servant, being born in the likeness of men. And being found in human form, he humbled himself by becoming obedient to the point of death, even death on a cross. Therefore God has highly exalted him and bestowed on him the name that is above every name, so that at the name of Jesus every knee should bow, in heaven and on earth and under the earth, and every tongue confess that Jesus Christ is Lord, to the glory of God the Father. (Phil. 2:5–11)

I encourage you take your time with these scriptures. Underline or highlight what Jesus' love for you motivated Him to do. And let it also motivate you to pursue love.

WORK IT OUT

> ❧ **To smile without fear of the future, I need to pursue love.** ❧

Pray 1 Corinthians 13:4–7:

> Dear Jesus, help me today to be patient and kind. Help me not to be jealous. I don't want to brag or be arrogant. Lord, help me not act rude. Help me not insist on my own way or be irritable or resentful. I do not want to rejoice at

wrongdoing, so help me rejoice with the truth. Jesus, today help me bear all things, believe all things, hope all things, and endure all things. Amen.

The thought patterns we entertain can produce more than momentary outbursts of anger or lapses in love. When we entertain resentment for any amount of time, it causes harm that requires repentance and forgiveness.

As you pray through these verses about love and dwell on God's love and His free gift of forgiveness for your sins today, ask Him to bring to your mind any person whom you have harbored resentment toward. Confess your sin. Ask God to forgive you and to help you forgive. Once you have done that, ask Him how you can show love to that person.

Day 5

Lady Wisdom

Memory Verse

Love _____ all things, _____ all things,
_____ all things, _____ all things.

1 Corinthians 13:7

The passage that details the character of the Proverbs 31 woman makes up an epilogue to the entire book. Proverbs is rich in its call to pursue wisdom and in the practical application of that path. Proverbs 31:10–31 has even been called "the ABCs of wisdom."[1] Draw a line to match each proverb below to the expression of wisdom in the verses about the Proverbs 31 woman.

Proverbs 8:11   "She watches over the affairs of her household and
                                 does not eat the bread of idleness" (v. 27 NIV).

Proverbs 19:15   "She opens her arms to the poor and extends
                                 her hands to the needy" (v. 20 NIV).

Proverbs 9:10   "A wife of noble character who can find? She is
                                 worth far more than rubies" (v. 10 NIV).

Proverbs 22:9   "Charm is deceptive, and beauty is fleeting; but a woman
                                 who fears the LORD is to be praised" (v. 30 NIV).

Proverbs 10:31   "She speaks with wisdom, and faithful
                                 instruction is on her tongue" (v. 26 NIV).

The Proverbs 31 woman mirrors Lady Wisdom. Lady Wisdom is the poetic personification of wisdom, and she speaks three times in the early chapters of Proverbs: 1:20–33; 8:1–36; and 9:1–6.

You may want to read some or all of these poems. As you do, you'll likely hear echoes of what you've learned about the woman in Proverbs 31. But Lady Wisdom is not alone. The first nine chapters of Proverbs do not discuss wisdom only; they also contrast the ways of wisdom with the ways of folly.

Read chapter 9 and answer the following questions.

What is the name of Lady Wisdom's opposite? How is she described? (v. 13)

Where are both Lady Wisdom and the woman Folly when they call to those who pass by? (vv. 3, 14)

What do both Lady Wisdom and the woman Folly say? (vv. 4, 16)

What happens to those who answer Lady Wisdom's call? (v. 6)

What happens to those who follow the woman Folly? (v. 18)

It's interesting that though the paths of wisdom and folly have such different outcomes, the way they begin their invitations is identical. I like how *The Message* paraphrases verses 4 and 6 of Proverbs 9:

> Are you confused about life, don't know what's going on?
> Come with me....
> Leave your impoverished confusion and *live*!
> Walk up the street to a life with meaning.

We won't always have all the answers. We won't always understand what is going on around us. In those moments, we fear the future. Instability and uncertainty trigger all the what-ifs about what may come.

In those moments, we can choose to remain confused and fear the future, or we can choose to leave that impoverished life and accept God's invitation to come with Him and live.

The paths of the woman Folly and Lady Wisdom sound a lot like chasing the world's version of Happy and pursuing love. One offers empty promises that lead only to disappointment and dissatisfaction. The other offers an invitation to experience the fullness of life.

The Proverbs 31 woman is a picture of a woman who guards her heart and her way. She lets God's Word inform her motives and motions. And because she does this, she smiles without fear.

WORK IT OUT

> ❧ **To smile without fear of the future, I need to pursue love.** ❧

Pray 1 Corinthians 13:4–7:

> Dear Jesus, help me today to be patient and kind. Help me not to be jealous. I don't want to brag or be arrogant. Lord, help me not act rude. Help me not insist on my own way or be irritable or resentful. I do not want to rejoice at wrongdoing, so help me rejoice with the truth. Jesus, today help me bear all things, believe all things, hope all things, and endure all things. Amen.

As you close out this week, ask God to show you any times you have followed the path of folly instead of wisdom or chased Happy instead of pursuing love. Ask Him to show you where you have not allowed His Word to inform your motives or your motions. Look up scriptures that can encourage and equip you to follow the path of wisdom in those places. Use the space below to note verses you find and how you can apply them in your life.

We can choose to remain confused and fear the future,
or we can choose to leave that impoverished life and
accept God's invitation to come with Him and live.

Love Target

Love is patient and kind;
love does not envy or boast;
it is not arrogant or rude. It does
not insist on its own way; it is not
irritable or resentful; it does not rejoice
at wrongdoing, but rejoices with the
truth. Love bears all things, believes
all things, hopes all things,
endures all things.

1 Corinthians 13:4–7

Video Session 5: Her Heart's Pursuit

Watch video session 5, and use this space to write notes or record insights.

_____
_____
_____
_____
_____
_____
_____
_____
_____
_____
_____
_____
_____
_____
_____
_____
_____
_____

Week 5

My Heart's Perspective: Living Intentional

✿

Memory Verse

Train yourself in godliness.

1 Timothy 4:7 CSB

Introduction

My hands gripped the wheel, and my body broke out in a sweat. Something wasn't right.

Just a few minutes before, we had frantically packed our lives into two trailers. We were moving … again. And we were running late … which was not unusual.

As a new football season approached, we were moving our home base from Texas all the way to an East Coast city in Florida. We had intended to be on the road already, but boxes and sofas and a lot of other things still littered the lawn. We didn't have time for a plan anymore, so we started throwing everything into the trailers.

With the lawn no longer covered in our things and with the kids secured into their car seats, Luke hopped behind the wheel of his truck, and I got in my car, and together we set off on the daylong trip. He went first, pulling a trailer, and I followed with a trailer as well.

The first left turn put us on a road we'd traveled many times in Luke's career. No matter where our journey took us, it always seemed that this road was the road that led home. We traveled it after winning seasons and after losing ones. We traveled it healthy, and we traveled it sick and injured. We traveled it overflowing with expectation, and we traveled it almost hopeless.

We knew this road well. That's why I was so startled.

Minutes into our trip, as I guided my car around a slight curve in the road, it felt like I lost control of the vehicle. I couldn't figure out why, but it happened again at the next curve. I knew I couldn't continue like this, so I called Luke and reported the problem.

He wanted to see for himself, so we pulled over, switched vehicles, and continued on our way. Sure enough, just a few minutes later, he hit a small bump in the road and felt the same thing. The vehicle felt out of control, but Luke knew exactly what was wrong.

"It's loaded wrong," he informed me. "We'll have to unload and start over."

In our haste to get on the road, we hadn't loaded the trailer correctly. The heavy things—sofas, chairs, and loaded-down boxes—should have gone in first. We should have thrown in the light things last. When we found ourselves running behind schedule, we didn't give thought to the right way to load. Consequently, the load was steering the vehicle instead of the vehicle steering the load.

A local post office's parking lot became the stage for the total unloading and reloading of our things. Some ladies crossed the street to get to us, thrilled at their luck in being the first at the garage sale. Post office personnel came out to tell us we couldn't have a yard sale on their lawn. We assured them all that we weren't setting up a sale, although I'm pretty sure Luke would have given it all to the highest bidder at that point.

After almost an hour, we (and when I say "we," I mean Luke) had the trailer unpacked and repacked, this time correctly. We piled back into our vehicles and set off down the road once again, this time in peace. No more white knuckles clenched around a wheel we couldn't control. No more fear of what the next bump in the road might bring.

I'm finding my heart isn't much different from that trailer.

Day 1

Developing a Spiritual Training Circle

Memory Verse

Train yourself in godliness.

1 Timothy 4:7 CSB

So often we see someone's end result. We see a couple celebrating fifty years of marriage or a person crossing the finish line of a marathon. We see a woman who smiles without fear and twenty-two verses that detail her life's work. We see a family pulling two perfectly loaded trailers into their destination.

The danger in viewing only the end result is that we can assume that the lives and situations we see all just kind of fell into place. But almost always, an end result is a result that required work—going through difficult times and suffering failures. It's a result that is the expression of intentional choices.

If last week we made a plan for how to direct our pursuits, then this is the week to make a plan for our plan. No matter how great our intentions, no matter how motivated we feel today, life sometimes takes our pursuits off track—way off track.

Living every day clothed with strength and dignity and smiling without fear requires more than just a good attitude. It will take more than a few weeks of Bible study. It's going to take strategic, intentional training.

Several words used to describe the Proverbs 31 woman are also used to describe armies or their activities. Consider the very first verse about her: "An excellent wife who can find? She is far more precious than jewels" (v. 10).

The Hebrew phrase translated "excellent wife" is *'ēšet-ḥayil*.[1] Depending on what translation of the Bible you read, you can find this phrase rendered a variety of ways: "capable wife" (HCSB), "wife of noble character" (NIV), "virtuous woman" (KJV), or "valiant woman" (JUB[2]).

Ḥayil is defined as "a force, whether of men, means or other resources"[3] and is frequently found in military contexts.[4]

Look up the verses below, and draw a line connecting each with the way *ḥayil* is used.

Judges 6:12	army
1 Samuel 17:20	forces
2 Kings 25:5	host
2 Chronicles 17:2	valor

Beyond that one Hebrew word, other verses in Proverbs 31:10–31 draw on military contexts as well:

Verse 11: "The heart of her husband trusts in her, and he will have no lack of gain." The Hebrew word translated "gain" is *shalal* and means "plunder" or "spoil."[5]

Verse 29: "Many women have done excellently, but you surpass them all." The final part of this verse can also be read "you ascend above," which usually refers to going out to battle.[6]

With such strong military overtones, it is likely that the author intended the reader to recognize warrior imagery in these verses.[7] Therefore, it seems fitting to spend some time considering the Proverbs 31 woman as a soldier enlisted in God's army to accomplish His purposes. In fact, when we consider the extent of her productivity, it's almost impossible to imagine that she could have accomplished so much apart from a well-ordered training plan.

DIGGING IN

Read 2 Timothy 2:3–4:

> Share in suffering as a good soldier of Christ Jesus. No soldier gets entangled
> in civilian pursuits, since his aim is to please the one who enlisted him.

According to these verses, what does a good soldier of Jesus *not* do?

Other translations render the expression "civilian pursuits" like this: "the [ordinary business] affairs of civilian life" (AMP), "worldly affairs" (TLB), or "the affairs of everyday life" (NASB).

Based on these descriptions, what are some things you would call "civilian pursuits"?

I found it difficult to wrap my mind around the idea of civilian pursuits. As it pertains to war and armies, I'm a civilian. I always have been. So I asked a few of my friends and family who have served in the United States armed forces. Their responses deeply affected me, and I want to share with you some of what they said:

> As a Marine, I had to be ready to fight at any given moment. I had to
> be in the best shape of my life, and also had to be available.... I used to
> train clearing rooms and buildings, dropped in by helicopter, night vision
> goggles, the whole nine yards. If I got called today to assemble a team to

go overseas and fight, I wouldn't be able to do it because I don't know a single person where I live who has that experience, training and readiness. I couldn't use anyone.

—Michael Frey, Retired, US Marines

As a soldier, I believe we are trained to be one-track-minded so that we would obey the orders given to us from higher. Our focus is the mission at hand.... I have always been under the impression nothing outside of the Army mattered to me.... The only thing that mattered to me is that we completed our mission and my soldiers all made it back safely.

—Adam Troy, Retired, US Army

Does anything jump out to you about how these two servicemen spoke about civilian pursuits? How does this change how you think about civilian pursuits?

I was deeply impacted by so many things these warriors said. Words like *ready* and *available*, *focus* and *mission*. I have read and reread this sentence: "The only thing that mattered to me is that we completed our mission and my soldiers all made it back safely." It has led me to search my own heart and ask myself, *What matters most to me? How concerned am I about the people around me hearing the gospel and arriving safely home in heaven?*

How would you answer those questions?

As we dive deeper into this idea of civilian pursuits and consider how being entangled in them affects our ability to smile without fear, let's read some of Jesus' words: "The worries of this life, the deceitfulness of wealth and the desires for other things come in and choke the word, making it unfruitful" (Mark 4:19 NIV).

We find this verse positioned within one of Jesus' parables. The seeds a farmer plants fall in different places—some along the path, some on rocky ground, some among thorns, and, finally, some in good soil. The seeds represent God's Word, and Mark 4:19 refers to those that fell among the thorns. Jesus said these are like people who hear the Word but, because of worries, wealth, or desires for other things, never bear fruit.

*To smile without fear of the future,
I need to live faithful today.*

I've read this parable many times, and when I get to this verse, I tend to skip the first thorn ("worries") and focus on the last two—the deceitfulness of wealth and the desires for other things. Somehow those seem more important to address or more likely to cause trouble.

But Jesus did not distinguish the worries of this life from the rest of the thorns.

The Amplified Bible renders "the worries of this life" as "the worries *and* cares of the world [the distractions of this age with its worldly pleasures]."

What would you say are some civilian pursuits you may be entangled in right now or have the tendency to become entangled in?

As long as we allow the worries of this life to entangle us, we risk being distracted by them, at best, and being consumed by them, at worst.

The Amplified Bible also says these thorns "creep in and choke out the word." This implies a kind of sneakiness to these civilian pursuits. They don't always announce themselves. Sometimes they slip into our hearts over time.

Finally, the worries of this life render us fruitless. They choke out whatever life and growth those good seeds would've otherwise produced. Becoming entangled in civilian pursuits appears to be the opposite of remaining in Christ. Civilian pursuits rob us of the sweet blooms of love and peace and gentleness, leaving us with withered hearts and depriving us of purpose.

Read the verses below; then underline the fruit of the Spirit.

> The fruit of the Spirit is love, joy, peace, patience, kindness, goodness, faithfulness, gentleness, self-control; against such things there is no law. (Gal. 5:22–23)

We are repeatedly reminded throughout Scripture that we cannot love both God and the world. They are enemies—two paths that lead in very different directions. Jesus said we will hate one and love the other. We will be devoted to one and despise the other (see Matt. 6:24). There's no neutral zone. We have to choose sides.

The fruit of the Spirit is love, joy, peace, patience, kindness, goodness, faithfulness, gentleness, and self-control. When we find that we are producing actions and emotions that are the opposite of these qualities, we could be entangled in civilian pursuits.

This brings us to our fifth and final step to becoming women who smile without fear of the future:

To smile without fear of the future, I need to live faithful today.

This week, we are going to develop what I call a spiritual training circle. It is designed to help us live faithfully every day as we train ourselves in godliness. It is to help us live ready and available, focused and on mission.

Our spiritual training circle will include four points: Scripture, community, prayer, and rest.

WORK IT OUT

> ✠ **To smile without fear of the future, I need to live faithful today.** ✠

The image of a spiritual training circle is drawn from the world of horse training. A horse is born with natural asymmetry. A natural bent to the left or right makes the horse imbalanced. If not corrected, this imbalance can lead to physical and behavioral problems.[8] One of the first steps to correcting this imbalance is the circle.

The circle exercise is intended to increase strength and flexibility and improve a horse's overall health. (Throughout this week, refer to the "Spiritual Training Circle" diagram at the end of the week.)

While it can seem monotonous and underwhelming, experts say that no exercise is more difficult than the circle. While young horses can run and even perform jumps, you never see a young horse perform an entire circle. "The reason a full circle is so difficult, is the natural asymmetry of the horse. A left bent horse has the tendency to lean in to the circle on the right and to lean out on the circle to the left."[9]

Consider your natural "bents" in light of the four points of our spiritual training circle—Scripture, community, prayer, and rest. Do any of these feel more like your natural bent than the others? List them here.

Just as young horses grow in physical health, for us to grow in spiritual health, we must work to train ourselves for godliness. So grab your water bottle, and put on your spiritual stretch pants. It's going to be a great week!

Day 2

That Thing You Keep Bringing Up

Memory Verse

Train yourself in _____.

1 Timothy 4:7 CSB

Every television channel we turned to was covering it. Every person we talked to had something to say about it. In fact, it seemed as if no one had much to say about anything else. Every direction we turned showed signs of people preparing for it.

It was a hurricane. And it was headed straight for us.

For a few years, Luke and I lived in New Orleans. Up until then we had mostly been inland dwellers, surrounded by land and hours away from any major body of water. Consequently, we had no idea what to do about hurricanes.

When we found ourselves in the midst of a hurricane warning, it became all we could talk about too. We called people who knew more about this than us, and heeding their warnings, we packed up some belongings, ordered dinner to go, and got on the road heading to a place far from the path of the looming storm.

As we develop a spiritual training circle this week, you may notice that there are not necessarily direct mentions of the things we've been talking about in Proverbs 31:10–31. But stick with me.

Since Proverbs 31:10–31 serves as a conclusion to the entire book of Proverbs, and since the Proverbs 31 woman functions as a picture of a life lived wisely, we can make some assumptions about what she does based on what we learn from other verses in Proverbs. And we will use these things as we move around our spiritual training circle.

Read Proverbs 4:23–26, and list the four parts of our bodies we can train:

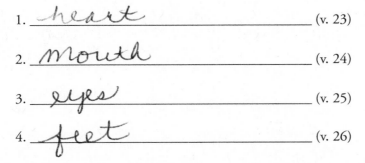

1. _heart_ _____ (v. 23)

2. _mouth_ _____ (v. 24)

3. _eyes_ _____ (v. 25)

4. _feet_ _____ (v. 26)

Proverbs 4 begins with a father's call to his sons to be attentive in order to gain wisdom and insight. These verses give us four imperatives to help us dedicate ourselves to training in godliness: the heart, the mouth, our eyes, and our feet.

We have talked extensively over the last four weeks about guarding and preparing our hearts. Last week we discussed how our hearts connect to our words. Today we will jump to number three on the list above: our eyes.

As we dive into the first point of our spiritual training circle—Scripture—we will see that in order to train our eyes in godliness, we must fix them on God's Word and His ways. We will also see a unique connection between our hearts, our mouths, and our eyes. Let's get into our first training exercise.

DIGGING IN

Read Hebrews 12:1–2:

> Therefore, since we are surrounded by such a great cloud of witnesses, let us throw off everything that hinders and the sin that so easily entangles. And let us run with perseverance the race marked out for us, fixing our eyes on Jesus, the pioneer and perfecter of faith. (NIV)

Circle what this verse tells us to throw off. Why does it tell us to throw off these things?

What does it tell us to do with our eyes?

These verses follow the chapter we spent some time in during week 3—Hebrews 11, known as the Hall of Faith. After the description of the cloud of witnesses, the word *therefore* at the beginning of Hebrews 12 encourages—even challenges—us to remember what they did so we, too, can run with endurance the race God has marked out for us. Then the writer of Hebrews tells us how to accomplish this—by fixing our eyes on Jesus.

The Greek word translated "fixing our eyes" is *aphoraō*, meaning "to turn the eyes away from other things and fix them on something."[1] It conveys the idea of a focal point that you do not take your eyes off of, even for a moment.

In high school I competed on the gymnastics team for a few years. Each meet included routines in four events—uneven bars, floor, vault, and balance beam. The balance beam was my weakest event. Something about being four feet off the ground with only four inches on which to put my feet made me nervous. My routine included turns, jumps, and even going upside down a time or two. I was always glad when it was over.

As unlikely as it sounds, I found that the key to staying on the beam from start to finish was my eyes. As long as my eyes stayed fixed on the beam, I had a focal point that kept me balanced. It was when I allowed my eyes to drift that my whole body began to waver.

A balance beam is a physical object—an easy thing to see and try to keep your eyes on. Fixing your eyes on Jesus may not seem as easy, since He is unseen. While we can't fix our eyes on the physical body of Jesus the way the disciples could while He walked on earth, the Bible gives us some clarity on how we can keep our eyes fixed on Jesus: "I will meditate on your precepts and fix my eyes on your ways" (Ps. 119:15).

In this verse, what did the psalmist say he would fix his eyes on?

Based on the beginning of this verse, how would he fix his eyes on God's ways?

In this verse the Hebrew word translated "I will meditate" is *siyach*, which means "to produce or bring forth" and carries the idea of rehearsing something in your mind.[2] It is a synonym of another Hebrew word, *hagah*, which literally means "to chew the cud."[3] Now, I'm a Texas girl, so this concept isn't as gross to me as it might be to you, but stick with me for a minute, and you'll see why this is important to understand.

To chew the cud refers to the digestion process of a cow (and some other grazing animals). When a cow starts to eat, it chews the food only long enough to get it soft. Then the food moves to the first of the cow's four stomach compartments, where it becomes what we call cud. Then the stomach muscles bring the cud back up to the mouth, where it is chewed again before being swallowed into the next stomach compartment for further digestion.[4] And now you know more than you ever thought you would about the digestive process of a cow.

We might say that *siyach* takes the image of chewing cud and applies it to our thoughts. To fix our eyes on Jesus, we can bring up God's Word in our thoughts and keep chewing on it in order to fully absorb and digest it.

A few verses later, the psalmist builds on this idea of his eyes: "Turn my eyes from looking at worthless things; and give me life in your ways" (Ps. 119:37). Just like the writer of Hebrews, the psalmist knew that in order to fix his eyes on God's ways, he would have to turn them from worthless things.

During those years in gymnastics, I learned that the key to success on the balance beam was to have a focal point. With each turn or flip, it was imperative that my eyes stayed fixed on a single spot on the four-inch apparatus. I couldn't take it lightly. To lose that focal point would almost ensure falling off and possible injury.

I want to treat Jesus this same way. This desire challenges me to prioritize the act of keeping my eyes fixed on Him, and it frees me to ignore everything that distracts me from Him.

Just before the psalmist declared that he would meditate on the instructions of the Lord, he tells us how this is possible: "I have stored up your word in my heart, that I might not sin against you" (Ps. 119:11).

What does this verse say the psalmist has done with God's Word? Why?

The picture of storing up God's Word brings a treasure chest to mind. It communicates the idea of taking something extremely valuable and storing it in a safe place. When you pair this verse with Psalm 119:16, you can see how the psalmist viewed God's Word. It wasn't something he forced himself to look at because he was supposed to do it or because he felt like he should. Instead, God's Word was a treasure to him. It delighted his soul.

My entire world is decorated with notes from my kids. On a shelf in my office, I have a note that says "I love you, Mom." The table next to my bed has artwork made just for me, and the refrigerator boasts recent and not-so-recent expressions of love from my little ones. I treasure these things because people I love made them with me in mind. Their expressions of love to me became a treasure and a delight—things I wanted to look at often.

Do you have any cards, notes, hand-drawn pictures, or something else that someone has given you that you display and look at often? Describe one here. What makes it so important to you?

The Bible is a book of inspired words from God's own heart. They are His revelation of Himself to us. When He breathed them, He had you and me on His mind. He wants us to know Him, so He gave us His words, His heart, and His plans in this book called the Bible.

I find it interesting that, between storing up God's Word in his heart and fixing his eyes on God's ways, the psalmist noted, "With my lips I declare all the rules of your mouth" (Ps. 119:13). This progression from heart to lips to eyes follows the pattern of Proverbs 4.

When the hurricane threatened New Orleans, what we saw dictated what we thought about. The images in front of our eyes refused to allow us to think about anything else. Our thoughts kept bringing up what our eyes saw, and what our thoughts kept bringing up, our mouths spoke about.

This hurricane was our "it." It was all we could see. It was all we could think about. It was all we could talk about.

Based on this discussion, what would you say is your "it" right now?

To smile without fear, we must live faithful today, and to live faithful today, we must train our eyes to stay fixed on Jesus. When God's Word is in front of our eyes, we can store it in our hearts. When we store it in our hearts, it will be on our minds. When we think about God's Word, we will talk about His Word. And when God's Word is what we keep bringing up, we will be one step closer to becoming women who smile without fear.

WORK IT OUT

> ✤ **To smile without fear of the future, I need to live faithful today.** ✤

Let's get very practical about our training in godliness. The goal is not simply to learn about these points on our spiritual training circle but to put them into practice so we will live faithful today.

List some of the things that cause you to be distracted. What things do you find yourself looking at instead of Jesus and His Word?

How will you intentionally fix your eyes on Jesus through His Word? Choose from the ideas in the box below, or write in some of your own ideas. I encourage you to not walk away from today's study until you have a plan for how you will fix your eyes on Jesus.

Pick a chapter in the Bible you'd like to begin reading. Each day read one to three verses of the chapter. Leave your Bible open so you can reread the verses several times throughout the day.	Store up Scripture in your heart by memorizing one verse a week (or every two weeks). Pick a verse, and divide it into easy-to-swallow phrases. Repeat one phrase over and over until you know it; then move to the next phrase.
Write down verses on note cards or sticky notes, and place them around your house or workplace. Pause to read these verses when you pass them, and remember all that you have to delight in through Jesus.	

Day 3

Watch Your Step!

Memory Verse

Train yourself in _godliness_.

1 Timothy 4:7 CSB

"Stay on the straight path."

I have such fond memories of a cartoon I used to watch with my kids when they were little. It involved two caterpillars and their adventures in a garden. They had ladybug friends and a spider friend. They helped a misbehaving bee and a lying fly learn to do right.

In one episode, their snail friend invited them to a party. The only instruction he gave them was to _stay on the straight path_.

The caterpillars started out fine, but sure enough, along the way there were many reasons why one of the caterpillars considered veering off course. A treat that looked tasty sat just off the path. An adventure that promised a good time called out for their attention. Finally, a shortcut proved too good to pass up.

As one caterpillar kept trying to veer off the straight path, the other caterpillar kept reminding him about the instruction: "Stay on the straight path." The first few times, he obliged, but eventually, when he was sure of the shortcut, he led his friend off a cliff. They slid down a slippery hillside and eventually tumbled into the party they were trying to reach—but not until the veggie dip bowl landed upside down on his head.

They did arrive at the party, but the road they took to get there was much more difficult than it would have been if they had just followed instructions and stayed on the straight path.[1]

When we read Proverbs 31, it can appear as though this woman needs no help. The landscape of our culture today feeds that way of thinking, making us more and more isolated and less and less connected. However, that's not at all what God's Word says.

While there isn't mention of a community that the Proverbs 31 woman meets with regularly or a friend who walks with her, this is, remember, an epilogue to the entire book of Proverbs. Therefore, we can assume she presents a complete picture of a wise woman, a woman who has shaped both her heart and her ways after God's wisdom. With that in mind, look up the verses listed below and draw a line connecting each to what it says about community.

Proverbs 12:15   Community sharpens us.
Proverbs 17:17   Community supports us in times of trouble.
Proverbs 27:17   Community can share wise counsel.

Before we continue, let's review the four imperatives found in Proverbs 4 that help us dedicate ourselves to training in godliness:

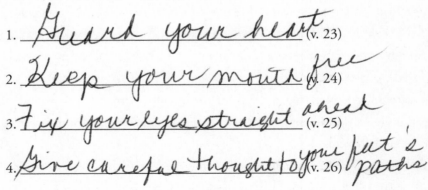

1. Guard your heart (v. 23)
2. Keep your mouth free (v. 24)
3. Fix your eyes straight ahead (v. 25)
4. Give careful thought to your feet's paths (v. 26)

Yesterday we saw how training our eyes relates closely to training our hearts and lips. Today we will move on to number four on our list: our feet. To smile without fear, we need to live faithful today, and living faithful today requires us to ponder the path of our feet, as noted in verse 26.

Pondering your path is proactive. One translation even words it, "Make the path for your feet level."[2] This implies intentionally choosing the way you will go and making a way to get there. Contrast that with what Proverbs 5 says about an adulterous woman: "She does *not* ponder the path of life; her ways wander, and she does not know it" (v. 6).

The path we choose for our feet will likely be influenced by the people we choose to bring with us, but it can also be influenced by the lack of them. At the She Laughs Conference, life coach and executive director of ministry training at Proverbs 31 Ministries Lisa Allen told about what her study of community has revealed. Here is one interesting quotation from John Ortberg that she shared:

> Researchers found that the most isolated people were *three times more likely to die* than those with strong relational connections.
>
> People who had bad health habits (such as smoking, poor eating habits, obesity, bad sleep habits, no exercise or excessive alcohol use) but strong social ties lived *significantly longer* than people who had great health habits but were isolated. In other words, it is better to eat Twinkies with good friends than to eat broccoli alone.[3]

In today's world, communication is at an all-time high yet connection is at an all-time low. We cannot confuse the two. Communication is merely the exchange of words. We can communicate without ever really connecting. Connection requires more from us, but it also provides more for us.

Today we will talk about point two of our spiritual training circle: community. *Community* may be defined as "a group of people living in the same place or having a particular characteristic in common."[4] As Christians, we have Jesus in common. He unifies us and directs us toward common attitudes and goals. We will see how community impacts the path of our feet and how important it is to our training in godliness and our goal of smiling without fear of the future.

DIGGING IN

Read the first sentence of Genesis 1:26:

> God said, "Let us make man in our image, after our likeness."

Circle or highlight the words *us* and *our*.

You may be wondering why in the world we are back in Genesis, but for us to understand the importance of community, I think it's vital for us to know where it came from. Community isn't man-made. In Genesis 1 we see whose idea this was. God exists as one being in three persons: the Father, the Son (Jesus Christ), and the Holy Spirit. There are fellowship and community in the very nature of God.

According to Genesis 1:26, how were we created?

If community is a part of the likeness of God and we are created in His likeness, then He designed us to exist in community as well. Therefore, community is a vital piece of our training in godliness. So let's see what we stand to gain when we engage in community.

Read Hebrews 3:13:

> Exhort one another every day, as long as it is called "today," that none of you
> may be hardened by the deceitfulness of sin.

What were these Christians told to do?

How often were they supposed to do it?

Why were they supposed to do it?

This verse gives Christians the charge to exhort one another. To exhort someone is to give an urgent, consistent, and strong form of encouragement. Notice that they weren't instructed to do it only once. They weren't even instructed to do it twice a week—on Sundays and at Bible study. They were instructed to do it every day.

Think for a minute about things you do every day. List some of those things.

I wonder if there is a person you talk to every day. Maybe it's your mom, spouse, sister, or coworker. Maybe you stop by the same coffee shop every morning, or maybe you watch television every night. Odds are, you pick up your cell phone every day to do something—send an email, check the weather, or scroll through social media. For most of us, daily life has regular aspects, like sleep and food.

This verse tells us something else to include in what we do every day—encouraging one another. With so many ways to communicate, we really don't have an excuse. We can send quick text messages just to check in. We can start a group on an app where we can share Bible verses and prayer requests. Now we even have the technology to call each other while we drive without even picking up the phone!

The biggest part of Hebrews 3:13, though, is what is at stake. These early Christians were instructed to exhort one another every day so that they wouldn't become hardened and deceived by sin. When we live in community, we are more guarded from our enemy. Remember the enemy we talked about in week 1, who seeks to steal, kill, and destroy us? We're safer together.

Read Proverbs 4:27: "Do not swerve to the right or to the left; turn your foot away from evil." With the final words of Proverbs 4, King Solomon essentially told his child, "Stay on the straight path." The wording of his instruction would have been familiar to the Hebrew hearer.

After Moses recounted the Ten Commandments to the nation of Israel, he counseled, "You shall not turn aside to the right hand or to the left" (Deut. 5:32). Just before Israel entered the Promised Land, Moses concluded the pronounced blessings for obedience with similar words: "If you do not turn aside from any of the words that I command you today, to the right hand or to the left" (28:14).

As Joshua stood poised to lead Israel into the Promised Land, God charged him to be "careful to do according to all the law that Moses my servant commanded you. Do not turn from it to the right hand or to the left" (Josh. 1:7). And as the end of Joshua's life drew near, he passed on God's command to Israel once again: "Be very strong to keep and to do all that is written in the Book of the Law of Moses, turning aside from it neither to the right hand nor to the left" (23:6).

The words of Proverbs 4:27 were passed down from generation to generation, and Solomon continued the teaching. Even the call to ponder the path of one's feet was given in community.

We too have the responsibility to continue the generational training in godliness. Wherever we have influence, we must be intentional and alert to opportunities to teach those behind us how to smile without fear and to extend to them the path of confidence, security, and purpose.

We're safer together.

WORK IT OUT

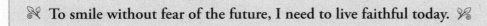

There are so many reasons why we resist engaging in community. People can be difficult. Demands of everyday life can be high. It may even feel as if no one wants to be in community with you. If you've ever been hurt by someone in the church, community becomes even more complicated.

This point of our spiritual training circle can be hard. That's why so many Scriptures about community urge us to bear with one another, forgive each other, and keep on loving one another (see Eph. 4:2; Col. 3:13; Heb. 13:1 NIV). All the things we learned about love last week apply here too. Engaging in community takes patience and endurance, and ultimately it takes the love of Christ being worked out in us and through us.

Is there a specific person or event in your life that causes you to resist engaging in community with other believers? Who or what is it?

If there is another reason you aren't interested in community, like time or availability, write that here.

Today I want to give you some ideas of how you can begin building community into your life. Look at the ideas that follow, and choose one or two things you can do to train yourself in godliness through community, or feel free to add your own ideas to the list.

Ask God to show you one or two ladies whom you can begin connecting with regularly through face-to-face meetups and daily accountability with texts, emails, or phone calls.	Look at your calendar, and determine a regular time that you can set aside to invest in people. You might find only one hour, but use the time God shows you to reach out and encourage people.
Commit to praying not only for God-honoring community in your life but also for the women all around you. As you begin to pray, watch how doors for community open up!	

Day 4

Something That Goes with Everything

Train yourself _in_ godliness

1 Timothy 4:7 CSB

The news felt heavy and almost devastating. As my sister looked at her little boy, she couldn't wrap her mind around the new landscape of the future. After months of tests and doctors' appointments, they had finally landed on the cause of all his illnesses.

Doctors diagnosed my nephew with a rare condition that involves his body not producing enough of the hormone cortisol. His production level was alarming. Cortisol connects directly to how our bodies handle stress, including sickness, injury, and any crisis situation. Cortisol has been called the body's "built-in alarm system."[1]

For most of us, our bodies respond to physical stress by instinctively producing two to three times the usual amount of cortisol.[2] But not my nephew. As my sister and my nephew learned more about his condition, they also learned measures they could take to prepare him in the event of sudden physical stress.

They got him an armband that he wears at all times. This armband serves as a sign of his condition for any medical personnel caring for him. In the event of an emergency, it will alert them of his needs immediately.

They also have a medical kit that stays with my nephew. The kit includes a way to inject stress doses of cortisol directly into his bloodstream. If he goes to swim practice, the kit goes with him. When he goes to school, the kit goes with him. When they go on vacation, the kit goes with him.

My sister doesn't want to wait for an emergency to start getting prepared. She knows his body's tendencies and insufficiencies, so she makes sure these things stay with him at all times.

Most things we do have limits. Most things we participate in have a season or term or perhaps an environment in which they are appropriate and other environments in which they are not so appropriate. Sledding and snow skiing don't work as well in summer months as they do in winter or early spring. A trip to the beach isn't the same during winter months as it is in the summer. We tend to notice when someone leaves Christmas lights up all year long, because it's the Christmas season for only a few weeks out of the year.

In yesterday's study, we listed some things we do every day. Go back and look at that list, and imagine if you did any of those things at all times. It probably wouldn't be good. There is one thing, however, that we can do all the time.

We can be "praying at all times in the Spirit, with all prayer and supplication" (Eph. 6:18). The verse goes on to say, "To that end, keep alert with all perseverance, making supplication for all the saints."

The Greek phrase translated "at all times" means … well, it means *at all times*. It's not often that we are given something to do and then told to do it at all times. Prayer, however, is one thing we are told to do at all times on every occasion.

Prayer goes with good days and bad days. Prayer goes with sickness and health. Prayer goes with certainty and uncertainty. Prayer goes with rejoicing and mourning. And did you notice how this verse connects prayer with community?

Who does it say to make supplication for?

Against the backdrop of the one thing that goes with everything, let's also consider the one thing that doesn't go with anything: "Do not be anxious about anything, but in every situation, by prayer and petition, with thanksgiving, present your requests to God" (Phil. 4:6 NIV).

What does this verse say we should not do?

When should we pray?

What should we pray with?

What should we do when we pray?

Now consider these two passages in Proverbs from the Amplified Bible:

> Lean on, trust in, *and* be confident in the Lord with all your heart *and* mind and do not rely on your own insight *or* understanding.
> In all your ways know, recognize, *and* acknowledge Him, and He will direct *and* make straight *and* plain your paths. (3:5–6 AMPC)

> Roll your works upon the Lord [commit and trust them wholly to Him; He
> will cause your thoughts to become agreeable to His will, and] so shall your
> plans be established *and* succeed. (16:3 AMPC)

Combining these passages with what you've read in Ephesians and Philippians today, consider what these verses teach us about prayer. In your own words, describe how prayer can affect everything we do.

So far this week, we've discussed how to train ourselves in godliness by making intentional choices to fix our eyes on God's Word and by connecting with other believers as we travel our daily paths. For the rest of this week, we will talk about two points of our spiritual training circle that impact our training in a different way. These points will help our training stay focused and productive.

To become women who smile without fear, we have to live faithful today. And as we will see, to live faithful today, we must pray at all times about everything.

DIGGING IN

Read Luke 5:15–16:

> But now even more the report about him went abroad, and great crowds
> gathered to hear him and to be healed of their infirmities. But he would
> withdraw to desolate places and pray.

This passage includes two instances of the word *but*. Circle them.

The first *but* draws attention to what was happening in the world around Jesus. Luke was basically saying, "Hey, look. The reports about Jesus' healings are spreading. Great crowds are coming to hear Him and be healed." Which makes the second *but* a little surprising. In spite of the growing crowds around Jesus, the Bible tells us His response was to withdraw from them. The NIV translation says, "But Jesus often withdrew to lonely places and prayed."

These lonely places were locations where Jesus could be alone with His Father, free from the distractions and demands of the world and even the demands of His disciples. These demands weren't necessarily bad, but they were demands for which Jesus knew He needed the power and presence of His Father. Jesus knew He needed to talk with His Father if He was to continue in the will of His Father. Therefore, Jesus slipped away—often—to places where He could be alone and pray.

Let's look at an example of a time when Jesus did this: "Perceiving then that they were about to come and take him by force to make him king, Jesus withdrew again to the mountain by himself" (John 6:15).

Circle the words *withdrew again*.

This verse immediately follows the miracle when Jesus fed more than five thousand people with only five loaves of bread and two fish. When the people witnessed this miracle, they wanted to exalt Jesus as an earthly king, so He withdrew. Matthew's account of this story adds the reason Jesus went to that mountain alone: "He went up on the mountain by himself *to pray*" (14:23).

We discussed earlier how prayer goes with all moments, and Jesus also demonstrated that. He prayed at what we might call some of His highest moments, after healings and other miracles, but He also prayed in the midst of what must have been one of His most difficult moments on earth. In the hours just before Jesus was tried as a criminal and crucified for the sins of all people, He went to the garden of Gethsemane with His disciples to pray.

> He withdrew from them about a stone's throw, and knelt down and prayed,
> saying, "Father, if you are willing, remove this cup from me. Nevertheless, not
> my will, but yours, be done." (Luke 22:41–42)

If Jesus needed to withdraw often and pray, no matter what situation He faced, then we can be sure this is a vital point of our spiritual training circle.

As we learn to train ourselves in godliness through prayer, I want to take a minute to talk about how prayer specifically relates to fear of the future. This is important because fear of the future can infiltrate our prayer lives and steal God's purpose for prayer.

While we most certainly can and should turn to God when we are afraid (as we learned in week 2), we don't want to let our fears fuel our fellowship with God. A few examples of how this might look include:

- Our requests become centered on protection. As we catalog all that could go wrong, we take each what-if to God and ask Him to help it not happen.
- Our prayers are short on—or completely lacking—thanksgiving. With our focus on our fears of the future, we miss all the blessings of the present.
- Our prayers focus on our circumstances instead of on God's glory.

Do any of these remind you of your prayer life? Do you struggle with one more than the others? Which one?

I don't want to pray just because I'm afraid—I want to pray because I believe. Because I believe in who God is and what He says.

When Jesus' disciples asked Him to teach them how to pray, He said, "When you pray, say: 'Father, hallowed be your name'" (Luke 11:2).

Jesus started His prayer with praise. I have invented a word for this kind of praying. I call it "prayse." I know that is technically a misspelled word, but I sometimes like to combine two words to make a new superword, and I think this is a great occasion for that.

When we start our prayers with praise to God, it becomes prayse. And when we prayse, we no longer filter God through our circumstances and make decisions about Him based on what we see happening around us. Instead, we filter our circumstances through God and make decisions about what we see happening around us based on what is true about Him. This one thing, friend, has been a game changer in my prayer life.

No matter what the future holds, when we train ourselves to begin our prayers with praise, we change our perspective. Instead of seeing a hopeless situation, we see the God who holds the situation. And when we see the future in the hands of our Father, we will become women who smile without fear.

WORK IT OUT

> ✄ **To smile without fear of the future, I need to live faithful today.** ✄

Praying at all times about everything is one of those ideas that can be easier said than done. It is not always our instinctive response to pray. That's why intentional training can be so helpful. Below is a list of ideas to help you move closer to this goal of praying at all times about everything—and praying because you believe, not because you are afraid. Choose a couple of these ideas, or write some of your own.

On sticky notes write things you want to pray about. Post them somewhere out of the way but where you will see them from time to time. I like to post them in my closet. Each time you pass one, stop and pray about what it says.	Set the alarm on your phone to go off two to four times a day. Label the alarm "Pray." Whenever it sounds, pray. Whether you are at the store, the gym, home, or work, pray. It doesn't have to be out loud or long, but for a moment direct your heart and mind to prayer.
Employ visual aids. Attach a person or situation to something you see. For example, if you have a friend who loves the color blue, pray for her every time you see that color.	

Day 5

Learning from the Master

Memory Verse

_____ _____ *in* _____.

1 _____ 4:7 CSB

As we conclude this study on becoming women who smile without fear, I can think of no better person to end it with than Jesus. We've spent time this week learning to look to Jesus and keep our eyes fixed on Him, and today we'll look to Him to learn about one final point of our spiritual training circle—rest.

Rest is a concept we don't always consider important. Sometimes we confuse rest with laziness. Sometimes we overindulge in rest and become lazy. But rest is a concept created by God—and Jesus invites us to rest. Therefore, it is a vital part of our success as we train ourselves in godliness.

> 28Come to me, all who labor and are heavy laden, and I will give you rest. 29Take my yoke upon you, and learn from me, for I am gentle and lowly in heart, and you will find rest for your souls. 30For my yoke is easy, and my burden is light. (Matt. 11:28–30)

What did Jesus invite the crowd to do? (vv. 28–29)

What will Jesus give to those who accept His invitation? (vv. 28–29)

How did Jesus describe His yoke? (v. 30)

Whom did Jesus call to come to Him? (v. 28)

This week may have felt intense to you. It may have even felt heavy. But as we just read, Jesus calls all who labor and are heavy-laden to come to Him and take His yoke.

Some scholars suggest that Jesus was referring to two kinds of loads. The word He used for "labor" points to the kind of load we place on ourselves, like the sickness of self-reliance we talked about in week 3. The word for "heavy-laden," however, points to loads placed on us by others.[1] The people in Jesus' original audience would have known well the burden of the mandates placed on them by the religious leaders of their day.[2]

What are some loads you are carrying right now that you have placed on yourself or that someone else has placed on you?

To those who chose to come to Him, Jesus offered rest for their weary souls. I love the way the Amplified Bible says it:

Come to Me, all you who labor and are heavy-laden *and* overburdened,
and I will cause you to rest. [I will ease and relieve and refresh your souls.]
(Matt. 11:28 AMPC)

In the next verse, the Amplified Bible defines this rest as "(relief and ease and refreshment and recreation and blessed quiet) for your souls."

A yoke in ancient times would have been tailor-made to fit so that it didn't choke or hurt the animal as it worked. A yoke was also often used to tie a younger, weaker animal together with an older, stronger one so that the stronger animal could carry the load while the weaker one learned.[3] When we come to Jesus and take His yoke on us, we can expect a yoke that is easy, well fitting, and light.

In Christ, we find relief and refreshment from the realities of today.

I hope, on this final day of our study together, your soul is less weary than it was when we began. But no matter how good today may be, the uncertainties of life require a place for us to find refreshment. Jesus promises us that place. In Christ, we find relief and refreshment from the realities of today.

Jesus broke the oppressive yoke of sin with His body and His blood so that we no longer have to bear that burden. His perfect love drives out fear (1 John 4:18 NIV), and He invites us simply to come to Him.

Come—the same word Jesus used when He called His disciples (see Matt. 4:19 NIV).

Come—the same word Jesus used in the parable of the wedding feast, inviting others to join Him (see Matt. 22:4).

Come—the same word Jesus used when He told about the day we will stand before God and He will invite us into eternal glory (see Matt. 25:34).

As we close our study together, it seems we've landed in the same place we began—with Jesus. He is our confidence. He is our security. He is our purpose. His victory is why we can smile without fear of the future. His Spirit is how we can apply these five steps to our lives.

WORK IT OUT

> ✂ **To smile without fear of the future, I need to live faithful today.** ✂

Go back to day 5 of each of the last four weeks, and review what you wrote on those days. How have you grown in your relationship with God over the last five weeks? Is there any one thing that has kept coming up throughout the study that you know God wants you to focus on? What is one thing you will do differently after having worked through this study? Use the space below to work through what you've learned.

_____

_____

_____

_____

_____

_____

_____

_____

_____

_____

_____

_____

He is our confidence. He is our security. He is our purpose.
His victory is why we can smile without fear of the future.

Spiritual Training Circle

Scripture

"I have stored up your word in my heart, that I might not sin against you."

Ps. 119:11

Rest

"Come to me, all who labor and are heavy laden, and I will give you rest."

Matt. 11:28

Prayer

"Do not be anxious about anything, but in every situation, by prayer and petition, with thanksgiving, present your requests to God."

Phil. 4:6 NIV

Community

"Exhort one another every day, as long as it is called 'today,' that none of you may be hardened by the deceitfulness of sin."

Heb. 3:13

Video Session 6: My Heart's Perspective

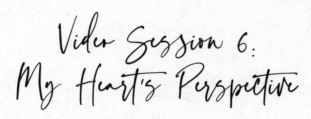

Watch video session 6, and use this space to write notes or record insights.

Conclusion

Little Did I Know

Last spring we decided to clean out some of the bookshelves at our house—a task long over-due. As Luke and I sifted through years' worth of books we had accumulated, I came across an old Bible. It wasn't a Bible I had used much, and I wondered why in the world I'd kept it all these years. Until I opened it.

There inside the front cover were three words that showed me the reason I still had this Bible. Against the background of a solid white page, nestled in the upper left-hand corner, were the words *Katy Griffin, Browns*.

I received this Bible at a summer camp put on by the Fellowship of Christian Athletes. At these camps, each person was assigned to a team—the group that person would huddle up with throughout the week to share about what he or she was learning. This particular summer, I wasn't Katy McCown *yet*, but I knew I wanted to be. I had recently graduated from college and started my television career, and I knew nothing—absolutely nothing—about the Cleveland Browns football team.

Little did I know, less than two years after this summer camp, I would be married to Luke McCown, the Cleveland Browns would draft my husband, and we would set off on our adventure together in the National Football League.

As I prepared to write this Bible study, I read this quote by John Piper that has become one of my favorites: "The future is the counsel of God being established. The future is the purpose of God being accomplished by God."[1] I think this quote explains why I still have a Bible from a summer camp that happened decades ago. It is an example of God's counsel being established in my life, and it reminds me that even when I don't see God at work, He is at work.

We can fully invest in today, confident that God will take care of tomorrow.

Remember that dreadful night when I collided with the cement post? I can still hear Luke's words: "I told you it wasn't raining." I can't help but think about how different the outcome would have been if I had just believed Luke when he told me that everything would be okay. I'm guessing I would have sidestepped the near face-plant that night.

When we trust what God tells us, we too can expect a different outcome. We can smile at the future, absolutely sure of God's control. We can fully invest in today, confident that God will take care of tomorrow.

Hear me, sister: that doesn't mean we'll never encounter fear of the future. There have been many nights when, with all the lights turned off and my head trying to rest on my pillow, fears of the future assault my thoughts. They threaten to take me captive. The difference is that now, when I begin to feel the grip of fear, I come back to these five steps.

To smile without fear of the future, I need to:

1. Spend less time *doing* and more time *being* with Jesus.
2. Exchange the *fear of the future* for the *fear of the LORD*.
3. Rely on my Savior instead of myself.
4. Pursue love.
5. Live faithful today.

As I recall each step, I ask myself, *Am I living each one of these? Which steps have I let fall by the wayside?* After I consider these questions, I make adjustments in my life to spend less time doing and more time being with Jesus, to pursue love, or to address whatever other step I may be neglecting.

With that in mind, I think it's time we go back to the very first day of our study. Five weeks ago, you may have left a couple of the blanks empty on day 1 of week 1. You may not have been ready yet to say that you are a woman who is clothed in strength and dignity and who smiles at the future. Today, though, I want you to go back to that page and consider it again.

By writing your name in the blanks, you are not declaring that you will get it right every time. You won't. You're not even declaring that you have it all figured out. You don't. You're not declaring that you are a model of strength and dignity to whom everyone from far and wide can look for answers. No, you are simply stating that you believe God. You believe what He said in His Word. You believe He has given you everything you need for life and godliness (see 2 Pet. 1:3), and you believe He is the author and perfecter of your faith (see Heb. 12:2).

In the introduction to this study, I shared with you some words from my journal:

> Jesus, I have these fears. Fears of the future. I'm scared. I know Your ways are
> not mine. I know they are good and far greater than anything I could fathom.
> I don't want to walk around shaky, anxious, fearful and distracted. Teach me
> how to live today.

Jesus did teach me how to live today. I pray that as I have shared what He taught me, you too can say He has taught you to live faithful today. I pray that you will no longer walk around shaky, anxious, fearful, and distracted but that you will instead live secure, confident, directed, and intentional. And I pray that as you live each day clothed with strength and dignity, you will smile without fear.

Notes

INTRODUCTION: I DIDN'T SEE THAT COMING

1. Julie Hanus, "Overcoming Fear Culture and Fear Itself," *Utne Reader*, January–February 2009, www.utne.com/politics/overcoming-american-fear-culture-on-eve-of-new-presidency.

2. "Impact of Fear and Anxiety," University of Minnesota, 2016, www.takingcharge.csh.umn.edu/impact-fear-and-anxiety.

3. Michael Foust, "Philippians 4:6 Was the Most Popular Bible Verse of 2019, YouVersion Says," ChristianHeadlines.com, December 5, 2019, www.christianheadlines.com/contributors/michael-foust/philippians-46-was-the-most-popular-bible-verse-of-2019-youversion-says.html.

WEEK 1, DAY 1: WHERE IS THIS COMING FROM?

1. Wendy Blight, *Living So That: Making Faith-Filled Choices in the Midst of a Messy Life* (Nashville: Thomas Nelson, 2014), 125.

WEEK 1, DAY 2: THE FIRST STEP TO SMILING WITHOUT FEAR

1. Bruce K. Waltke, *The Book of Proverbs: Chapters 15–31* (Grand Rapids, MI: Eerdmans, 2005), 520.

2. "Minerals and Metals," in *Tyndale Bible Dictionary*, ed. Walter A. Elwell and Philip W. Comfort (Wheaton, IL: Tyndale, 2001), 897; "Minerals, Metals, and Precious Stones," in *Baker Encyclopedia of the Bible*, ed. Walter A. Elwell (Grand Rapids, MI: Baker, 1988), 2:1466.

3. "Ruby," in *The Lexham Bible Dictionary*, ed. John D. Barry, rev. ed. (Bellingham, WA: Lexham, 2016).

4. Duane A. Garrett, *The New American Commentary: An Exegetical and Theological Exposition of Holy Scripture*, ed. E. Ray Clendenen, vol. 14, *Proverbs, Ecclesiastes, Song of Songs* (Nashville: B&H, 1993), 247.

5. Timothy Keller and Kathy Keller, *God's Wisdom for Navigating Life: A Year of Daily Devotions in the Book of Proverbs* (New York: Viking, 2017), 96.

WEEK 1, DAY 3: A PLACE WHERE YOU CAN BE SAFE

1. Bruce K. Waltke and Cathi J. Fredricks, *Genesis: A Commentary* (Grand Rapids, MI: Zondervan, 2001), 95.

2. Kenneth A. Mathews, *The New American Commentary: An Exegetical and Theological Exposition of Holy Scripture*, ed. E. Ray Clendenen, vol. 1a, *Genesis 1–11:26* (Nashville: Broadman & Holman, 1996), 254.

3. "Strong's G3306—Menō," Blue Letter Bible, 2020, www.blueletterbible.org//lang/lexicon/lexicon.cfm?Strongs=G3306&t=ESV.

4. "Repetition," Literary Terms, accessed May 16, 2020, https://literaryterms.net/repetition.

WEEK 1, DAY 4: UNINVITED GUESTS

1. "Strong's H5341—Natsar," Blue Letter Bible, 2020, www.blueletterbible.org//lang/lexicon/lexicon.cfm?Strongs=H5341&t=ESV.

WEEK 2, DAY 2: THE GREAT EXCHANGE

1. Edward W. Goodrick and John R. Kohlenberger III, *Zondervan NIV Exhaustive Concordance*, 2nd ed. (Grand Rapids, MI: Zondervan, 1999), 1493.

2. "Strong's H157—'Ahab," Blue Letter Bible, 2020, www.blueletterbible.org//lang/lexicon/lexicon.cfm?Strongs=H157&t=ESV.

WEEK 2, DAY 3: DO YOU KNOW OR DO YOU *KNOW*?

1. "Strong's G6063—Oida," Blue Letter Bible, 2020, www.blueletterbible.org//lang/lexicon/lexicon.cfm?Strongs=G6063&t=ESV.

2. "Strong's G1097—Ginōskō," Blue Letter Bible, 2020, www.blueletterbible.org//lang/lexicon/lexicon.cfm?Strongs=G1097&t=ESV.

WEEK 2, DAY 5: A WOMAN WHO FEARS THE LORD

1. *The Voice Bible*, copyright © 2012 Thomas Nelson, Inc., The Voice™ translation © 2012 Ecclesia Bible Society. All rights reserved.

WEEK 3, INTRODUCTION

1. "Triple Crown Fast Facts," CNN, June 24, 2020, www.cnn.com/2013/09/28/us/triple-crown-fast-facts/index.html.

2. *Secretariat*, directed by Randall Wallace (Burbank, CA: Walt Disney Pictures, 2010).

WEEK 3, DAY 1: UNLIMITED STRENGTH

1. "Strong's H5797— `Oz," Blue Letter Bible, 2020, www.blueletterbible.org//lang/lexicon/lexicon.cfm ?Strongs=H5797&t=ESV.

2. "Strong's H1926—Hadar," Blue Letter Bible, 2020, www.blueletterbible.org//lang/lexicon/lexicon.cfm ?Strongs=H1926&t=ESV.

3. "Names of God in the Old Testament," in *Faithlife Study Bible*, ed. John D. Barry (Bellingham, WA: Lexham, 2016).

WEEK 3, DAY 2: THE SECRET TO STRENGTH

1. "Strong's G2744—Kauchaomai," *Blue Letter Bible*, 2020, www.blueletterbible.org//lang/lexicon/lexicon.cfm ?Strongs=G2744&t=ESV.

2. "Strong's G769—Astheneia," *Blue Letter Bible*, 2020, www.blueletterbible.org//lang/lexicon/lexicon.cfm ?Strongs=G769&t=ESV.

WEEK 3, DAY 3: THE RELIEF OF RELYING ON GOD

1. Duane A. Garrett, *The New American Commentary: An Exegetical and Theological Exposition of Holy Scripture*, ed. E. Ray Clendenen, vol. 14, *Proverbs, Ecclesiastes, Song of Songs* (Nashville: B&H, 1993), 250.

2. Bruce K. Waltke, *The Book of Proverbs: Chapters 15–31* (Grand Rapids, MI: Eerdmans, 2005), 516.

3. James Swanson, *A Dictionary of Biblical Languages: Hebrew*, 2nd ed. (Bellingham, WA: Logos Research Systems, 2001).

4. "Nik Wallenda Completes Tightrope Walk across Gorge near Grand Canyon," CBS News, June 24, 2013, www.cbsnews.com/news/nik-wallenda-completes-tightrope-walk-across-gorge-near-grand-canyon.

5. Richard Pratt, *1 & 2 Chronicles: A Mentor Commentary* (Fearn, UK: Mentor, 2006), 404–5.

6. The MESSAGE Bible.

7. Pratt, *1 & 2 Chronicles*, 62.

WEEK 3, DAY 4: WHEN YOU COME TO THE END OF YOUR ROPE

1. Lexico.com, s.v. "counterfeit," 2020, www.lexico.com/en/definition/counterfeit.

WEEK 3, DAY 5: PEOPLE WHO DID THE IMPOSSIBLE

1. "Nobody," featuring Matthew West, track 2 on Casting Crowns, *Only Jesus*, Provident, 2018.

WEEK 4, DAY 1: CHASING HAPPY

1. GOD'S WORD Translation®, © 1995 God's Word to the Nations. Used by permission of God's Word Mission Society.

2. "Strong's G3512—Neōterikos," Blue Letter Bible, 2020, www.blueletterbible.org//lang/lexicon/lexicon.cfm ?Strongs=G3512&t=ESV.

WEEK 4, DAY 2: TARGET PRACTICE

1. "Strong's G3114—Makrothymeō," *Blue Letter Bible*, 2020, www.blueletterbible.org//lang/lexicon/lexicon.cfm ?Strongs=G3114&t=ESV.

2. "Strong's G5278—Hypomenō," *Blue Letter Bible*, 2020, www.blueletterbible.org//lang/lexicon/lexicon.cfm ?Strongs=G5278&t=ESV.

3. See, for example, Proverbs 31:18 in the English Standard Version.

4. Bruce K. Waltke, *The Book of Proverbs: Chapters 15–31* (Grand Rapids, MI: Eerdmans, 2005), 526–27.

5. "Gill's Exposition—Proverbs 31," Bible Hub, accessed May 22, 2020, https://biblehub.com/commentaries/gill /proverbs/31.htm.

6. Tremper Longman III, *Proverb* (Grand Rapids, MI: Baker Academic, 2006), 540.

WEEK 4, DAY 3: THREE WAYS TO PURSUE LOVE

1. Allen P. Ross, quoted in David Guzik, "Proverbs 31—The Wisdom of King Lemuel," Enduring Word, 2020, https://enduringword.com/bible-commentary/proverbs-31.

2. David Hubbard, *Mastering the Old Testament: A Book-by-Book Commentary by Today's Great Bible Teachers,* ed. Lloyd J. Ogilvie, vol. 15a, *Proverbs* (Dallas, TX: Word, 1989), 477.

3. Bruce K. Waltke, *The Book of Proverbs: Chapters 15–31* (Grand Rapids, MI: Eerdmans, 2005).

4. Hubbard, *Proverbs*, 484.

5. The Good News Translation in Today's English Version—Second Edition. Copyright © 1992 by American Bible Society. Used by permission.

WEEK 4, DAY 4: WHO WILL THINK OF ME?

1. "Strong's H7200—Ra'ah," Blue Letter Bible, 2020, www.blueletterbible.org/lang/lexicon/lexicon.cfm ?Strongs=H7200&t=ESV.

2. Timothy Keller and Kathy Keller, *God's Wisdom for Navigating Life: A Year of Daily Devotions in the Book of Proverbs* (New York: Viking, 2017), 83.

WEEK 4, DAY 5: LADY WISDOM

1. Allen P. Ross, "Proverbs," in *The Expositor's Bible Commentary*, ed. Tremper Longman III and David E. Garland, rev. ed., vol. 6, *Proverbs–Isaiah* (Grand Rapids, MI: Zondervan, 2008), 246.

WEEK 5, DAY 1: DEVELOPING A SPIRITUAL TRAINING CIRCLE

1. Bruce K. Waltke, *The Book of Proverbs: Chapters 15–31* (Grand Rapids, MI: Eerdmans, 2005), 516.

2. The Holy Scriptures, Jubilee Bible 2000 (from the Scriptures of the Reformation), trans. and ed. Russell M. Stendal. Copyright © 2013, 2020, by Ransom Press International.

3. "Strong's H2428—Chayil," Blue Letter Bible, 2020, www.blueletterbible.org//lang/lexicon/lexicon.cfm ?Strongs=H2428&t=ESV.

4. Waltke, *Book of Proverbs*, 516.

5. "Strong's H7998—Shalal," Blue Letter Bible, 2020, www.blueletterbible.org//lang/lexicon/lexicon.cfm ?Strongs=H7998&t=ESV.

6. Waltke, *Book of Proverbs*, 516.

7. Tremper Longman III, *Proverb* (Grand Rapids, MI: Baker Academic, 2006), 542.

8. "Every Horse Is Unique," Straightness Training, accessed May 25, www.straightnesstraining.com/natural -asymmetry/every-horse-is-unique.

9. "Circle," Straightness Training, accessed May 25, 2020, www.straightnesstraining.com/straightness-training -exercises/circle.

WEEK 5, DAY 2: THAT THING YOU KEEP BRINGING UP

1. "Strong's G872—Aphoraō," Blue Letter Bible, 2020, www.blueletterbible.org//lang/lexicon/lexicon.cfm ?Strongs=G872&t=ESV.

2. "Strong's H7878—Siyach," Blue Letter Bible, 2020, www.blueletterbible.org//lang/lexicon/lexicon.cfm ?Strongs=H7878&t=ESV.

3. "Chew the Cud," New Direction Bible Fellowship, accessed May 25, 2020, www.ndbf.church/wp-content /uploads/2018/02/Lesson-3-Pt2.pdf.

4. "What Is Cud, and Why Do Cattle Chew It?," Cattle Empire, December 20, 2013, www.cattle-empire.net /blog/f/what-is-cud-and-why-do-cattle-chew-it.

WEEK 5, DAY 3: WATCH YOUR STEP!

1. "Hermie & Friends Short: Buzby Straight," Tommy Nelson, video, www.youtube.com/watch?v=7NGjq0UyTrk&t.

2. The NET Bible®, copyright © 1996, 2019 by Biblical Studies Press, LLC. http://netbible.com. All rights reserved.

3. Ronald Weisel II, "It Is Better to Eat Twinkies with Good Friends Than to Eat Broccoli Alone," Hartville Health and Wellness Centre, April 21, 2011, https://hartvillehealthandwellness.com/nutrition/it-is-better -to-eat-twinkies-with-good-friends-than-to-eat-broccoli-alone.

4. Lexico.com, s.v. "community," 2020, www.lexico.com/en/definition/community.

WEEK 5, DAY 4: SOMETHING THAT GOES WITH EVERYTHING

1. "What Is Cortisol?," WebMD, accessed May 26, 2020, www.webmd.com/a-to-z-guides/what-is-cortisol#1.

2. "Addison's Disease," Mayo Clinic, October 9, 2019, www.mayoclinic.org/diseases-conditions/addisons-disease /symptoms-causes/syc-20350293.

WEEK 5, DAY 5: LEARNING FROM THE MASTER

1. David Guzik, "Matthew 11—Not the Messiah They Expected Him to Be," Enduring Word, 2018, https://enduringword.com/bible-commentary/matthew-11.

2. R. T. France, *The Gospel according to Matthew: An Introduction and Commentary* (Grand Rapids, MI: Eerdmans, 1985), 200.

3. William Barclay, *Gospel of Matthew*, rev. ed. (Louisville, KY: Westminster John Knox, 2001), 20–21.

CONCLUSION: LITTLE DID I KNOW

1. John Piper, "The Sovereignty of God: 'I Will Accomplish All My Purpose,'" Desiring God, November 3, 2012, www.desiringgod.org/messages/the-sovereignty-of-god-my-counsel-shall-stand-and-i-will-accomplish-all -my-purpose.

She Smiles without Fear

Video Session Access

One introductory video
and five lesson videos

Link: **https://lesson-dl.com/**

Access code: 1504639

See Katy Live!

If you were inspired by *She Smiles without Fear* and desire to share this with others in your community, we have just what you're looking for.

At the She Laughs Conference, Katy joins with other dynamic speakers to come to *your church* for two sessions packed full of laughter, encouragement and sound Biblical teaching. Through intimate conferences in local churches around the world, we use God's Word to find practical answers to today's most pressing questions about freedom, security and purpose.

Learn more and schedule your conference today at **shelaughsconference.com**.

Connect with Katy at www.katymccown.com or on social media @katymccown.